12/12/89 - 2/14/15

r.i.p lil dave

PHOTOFY

I'm Alive

iUniverse books may be ordered through booksellers or by contacting:

iUniverse
1663 Liberty Drive
Bloomington, IN 47403
www.iuniverse.com
844-349-9409

ISBN: 978-1-6632-5231-9 (sc)
ISBN: 978-1-6632-5232-6 (hc)
ISBN: 978-1-6632-5217-3 (e)

Library of Congress Control Number: 2023906641

Print information available on the last page.

iUniverse rev. date: 05/09/2024

I'M ALIVE

By:

Wendy

http://wendylarramore.site/
http://bbbchurch.net

This book is not perfect. I do have a traumatic brain inury.

Contents

Chapter 1: Childhood life

It all started on July 25th, 2012. I don't know why but I ran the red light at 103rd and Chaffee. I live in Jacksonville Florida on the west side, Duval. My fiancée at the time (Chuck) said I was texting him and his reasoning was I had a text to him on my phone but whatever. My phone was dead when they found it, so I was either texting or plugging it in. I have been known to text and drive. I've also been known to play games on my phone while driving. Do not text and drive, look at me. I ran into a semi-truck carrying a 90 thousand lb. cement pole. It then jackknifed and hit me again. I (unconscious) was transported to Orange Park Hospital. After a few weeks with no response, they talked my family into sending me to hospice. When it comes to the grim reaper, he doesn't know me too well, obviously. They were saying that I had brain damage in the occipital lobe. The back part of your brain that controls your consciousness. They said I would never wake up. After sending me to die at hospice, I woke up after 5 days with no food or water. They tried to starve me to death. I showed them, I wasn't ready to die. I think that's why I woke up and I woke up loving food. My foot was almost torn completely off. I went to Shans Hospital after hospice. They put rods in my leg. I have two big ones and a little one. I'm lucky I can walk at all. During my hospital visit I was never alone. Someone was there with me around the clock. My cousin Silvia said she had never seen so many people in the same room praying for someone. Well, it worked look at me now. I'll tell you about my recovery and how my family helped me, after I tell you a little about my recovery childhood life and up to the time of my accident.

I am the youngest and only girl; I have four older brothers. My mom and dad (John and Alta) Adams raised us very religiously. My Dad is a deacon at our blanding Baptist church, Blanding Blvd Baptist. Dr. David Strunk was the pastor then and Dr. David Adear is the pastor now. I kind of feel bad because I know that God saved my life and I'm not doing anything to thank him. I know I should have died that day. Maybe I'm serving him by writing this book and becoming physical therapist for other people like me. I just don't feel I'm called for anything as of yet. They knew right away I had all my memories because even before I opened my eyes my brother Steven asked me to give dad a piggy kiss and I did. I guess I gave a lot of them when I was little because I remember them talking about them.

Joel being my oldest brother. I remember him being like the babysitter. He was always in charge. He was off in the service before I was in my teens. The air force took him to Amsterdam for 16,17 years. He just moved back a year or two before my accident. He moved back with a wife (Tonja) and daughter (Naomi). Paul is my second oldest brother. He was my goofy funny brother. His name is actually John Paul Adams. He was named after my dad, John. He always picked fights between me and my youngest brother, Stephen. He thought it was funny. He lives in New Mexico now, Silver City. His ex-wife moved back home to be with her family. That was the only way he could be with his kids. What can I say he is a good father! He was in the Army. He has Vanessa, Holly, Amanda, Jonathan, and Destiny. Destiny isn't his, but we won't get into that, we claim and love her anyway.

David is my second youngest brother. He was always the one that kissed my boo boos. It's kind of weird how it turned out because he was the one into sports. You would have thought he was healthy. He had a stroke the year before my accident, I think. I'm still not good with my timing. He is with Sue now. I found out she is a really sweet person. She helped me out tremendously after my accident. She is a wedding planner by profession. She helps her best friend, Tawnee. Tawnee owns a wedding planner business. They made my wedding day beautiful.

I had Miranda as my matron of honor. Then as bride's maids I had Dana, Ashley and Chuck's cousin Tracy. Chuck and Tracy grew up together. So, they're more like brother and sister. If I had the money, I would buy a second house in Lakeland. Right on the Lake. There would be horses, pigs, goats and chickens. I would like for it to have a rental property. In the main house I would like two master bedrooms and a big front porch and back porch. I also would like a mudding spot close by. What can I say I am a Redneck. you got to have some mud. Maybe we can just find a big piece of land and I can build houses on it. When I was a teenager, I use to go around drawing up plans for houses. I would love to actually build a few. I know it's a Lake house, but I got to have a pool. I would love to have a custom pool. One that I see on my HGTV show I watch in the wee hours of the morning. The infomercials. I seem to watch a lot of infomercials. I would let Chuck decorate it the way he likes. I kind of took over our house in Jacksonville. Back to the story Wendy. There I go getting off track again. Chuck had Donald for his best man. Mike, Brian, and Ray for the groomsmen. As the first dance, we danced to "God gave me you" It was beautiful! I thought it was so appropriate. It couldn't have been more perfect. It was at the Lakeshore Women's Club right on the St. Johns River. It was beautiful!

Next is my youngest brother, Stephen. I always got into fights with him. I was one tough little girl. I think I survived because I was tough. Me and him used to get into some knockdown, drag out fights. I think he had to prove that he could win. Paul always said Stephen gets beat by a girl. He is married to Dee now. I have been friends with her since I was a kid. I remember her saying that I had sores everywhere but my face. I could never have my face messed up. I was always into the way I looked. I have natural curly hair. Everyone always says I have beautiful hair. IDK, I'm just the girl with brown curly hair. I have one rule; you can skimp on almost anything, but you can't skimp on your hair products. My brother Stephen taught me that. When he was in his late teens went through a stage where he grew his hair out long. It was all fried and frizzy. Then one day I seen him, and it was healthy and beautiful. His hair is darker than mine. I wish my hair looked like his did. He shaves his hair now, a buzz cut. He says it's cheaper and easier.

My only wish is to give me a product for my thinning hair. Well, I shouldn't say only. That's were Karatic hair loss would come in real handy. I would love to try vivisacal too. I used to love this product that Pantene had. It was a leave on conditioning spray for curly hair. I had it before my youngest was born and I'm still pining away over it now. I would do anything to get that product back. Well, I shouldn't say anything. Almost anything sounds better. I want to try Wen hair products. It has to be good, it's named after me. Just kidding but they do have the first three letters of my name. It's supposed to eliminate the usage of all other hair products. Now that's exciting. I glop so many hair products in my hair it's terrible and it usually drips on my shirt. I'm a mess. When I got to the hospital my hair was all matted from the blood, so mom decided to cut it all off. Peroxide gets blood out, but what better time to cut it all off. It's definitely healthier now. Now that I think about it, peroxide would have most likely have hurt, they probably thought I have already been through enough. My hair won't grow out long for some reason. I can't get it to grow past my shoulders, even though I have never had my hair long, even before my accident. Maybe a product that will help me grow my hair long would be really nice. I would love to try Cindy Crawford, meaningful beauty. I would love to have the Spin Spa. I have a knock off version now. Anything that helps me be younger and more beautiful. I also would like to try Bye Bye foundation and cosmetics. I have a rather large freckle on the side of my eye. Someone once called it a greckle. I've been self-conscience of it ever since. Funny, I never even paid attention to it before that. I would like to try Dermaflash. That seems like it would work really well. She (Dee)has two kids prior to Steven. Janelle and Amber. They are I think 18, and 20. I'm here to tell you God knew what he was doing when he made me. It's like I was bread with four older brothers to make me tough. I found out with my last hospital visit I have a high tolerance to pain. Even the determination I got from my dad is all planned out. I was born and raised in a God loving home even the church I go to is part of Gods big plan.

I remember spending a lot of my time with my cousin and at the time my best friend Michelle Eiland. My mom's brother is her dad, Uncle Gene. Uncle Gene was married to Aunt Pat. She passed away last year. She always took Michelle and I shopping. Michelle and I are still good friends today. My mom has another brother, John Lee. Him and my dad were good friends and was in the service together. He was married to Aunt Jeannie. My Aunt Jeannie passed away and so did my cousin Scott. They had 5 children together, including Scott. My mom had one older sister, Aunt Frieda. She was blessed with four boys. Tommy is the exterminator. He keeps the family bug free. I remember hanging out at his house growing up and during my first marriage. I saw all of his kids grow up. They call me Aunt Wendy even though I am his cousin. I feel kind of bad because when Tommy separated, I stopped getting to see

Nikki, all the rest of them came to see Tommy. But for some reason not Nikki. I just got to see her the other day. She has become a beautiful young lady with a bunch of children I don't even know. I should have made a point to see more of her. I'm an adult. I'm kind of partial when it comes to Cecili. She has the perfect personality and she's pretty. Beautiful inside and out. Sort of what I would like to be. I am worried about Aunt Frieda. She's not doing too good. She stays in her home most of the time. I grew up on Elm Grove Ave. with my brothers and cousins. My granddad owned one side of the little dead-end road; I made a lot of memories there. My Grandpa and dad built our house. Well, their house really (mom & dads). They sold the properties of the road little by little. Most of my aunts and Uncles lived there. All except Uncle John Lee and his family. They lived in Chiefland. About an hour away. As you can tell, having four older brothers and a family owning half of the street. I was one girl who thought she owned the street. I was a prissy little girl. I only used my brothers as an excuse a one time. It didn't work. I didn't do that anymore. I told the guy my 4 brothers are going to beat you up; he ended up being friends with Stephen. After that I just learned to fight my own battles.

My dad's side of the family was very large. He had three brothers and four sisters. There's Uncle Richard, Uncle Anthony with his wife and two girls. Then there is Uncle Philip with his three kids. My Uncle Philip passed away. There are four girls. My dad's sisters are Aunt Joanne, Aunt Carolyn, Aunt Margie and Aunt Darrel. Aunt Margie passed away when I was young. That was the first funeral I ever went to. They had three girls. My Aunt Joanne was married to Uncle Randy. They had 4 children. They both passed away. My Aunt Carolyn is married to Uncle Don. They had two boys. They lived in Washington DC while I was growing up until their kids were grown. They visited every couple of years. Then they finally moved back. It's Funny how things turn out. The first memory I have is of them buying me my Winnie the pooh doll at Disney world. I still have it today in my memory box. I found out much later that my parents paid for it. They (Aunt Carolyn and Uncle Don) taking me to spend time with me. Anyway, when I was in the hospital, they brought me a stuffed frog. I didn't know they brought me that frog until mom told me much later. I slept with that stupid frog for a long, long time after my accident. That frog still has a spot on my bed today.

I got my G.E.D. close to my 18th birthday. Then after I got married in May of 1991. I had two children, Ray-Ray and Ashley. Stayed married for 9 long years. And then I met a cute surfer boy about 2 years after my divorce and I ended up pregnant. What can I say he was cute! I think I was in lust. That goes to show you God knows what is best for you. I wasn't very religious during my marriage and until the time of my accident. Except when I got pregnant. I was going down the wrong path before I got pregnant, I was kind of wild. I had to quit everything. We broke up and I never seen him again. That proves that God knows what you need. After my divorce, I started college and I worked three part-time jobs. One as a waitress in a bar, one as a housekeeper (I had 2 houses I cleaned) one of the houses I had for like 11 years, Mrs. Howard, and one as a CNA or caregiver. I worked for Charlie and Mary Stringfellow for like 9 -or 10 years. A long time anyways. Until they both passed away. Mary passed away first. She is who I was hired to take care of, well take shopping really. She had COPD and was on oxygen. Then I took care of Charley. He had a pig valve in his heart. It only lasts for ten years once the ten years is up it's up. Anyway, Mayo Clinic said the only chance he had was to have heart surgery. At 91, yeah right. He passed away a couple of days after the surgery. I was attached and cared for them both dearly. I was treated very good by his son Charlie Stringfellow the second. He ended up paying me generously to help clean out their house and to keep it clean. I would say Mary was a pack rat but that wouldn't be very nice. She was very clean but had a big house and put it all up neatly. She just liked to shop, that's all. Well, IDK, she had every card that was ever given to her.

After that was done, I got a job at Apex, as a CNA. I made ends meet until I moved in with Chuck. He saved me. I met Chuck before my youngest was 2. He's 11 now. He has raised him as his own. He's a good dad. He's strict and spends a lot of time teaching him. He is strict but not abusive. I kind of feel bad because my other two didn't get the discipline and responsibility that Joshua is getting.

Ashley has her man that pays her bills. Ray Ray has to pay all his own bills. I should of took more time to teach him money management. I know he can do it, he moved out one time. It was when he lived with me. He moved in with his friend. Rented out a room. I found out Ray Ray stood up for Chuck when they put me in hospice. I'm proud of him. I guess people don't act all that good when someone you love is dying. God says thou shalt not judge. So, I don't judge. I'm not perfect but at least I'm not judgmental. I'm not hypocritical. Chuck don't want to talk about it, so I really don't know what even happened anyway. Ray Ray has never been in trouble with law so that's a good positive. I always had a flat belly after my first two pregnancies. I wore the same size pants as before the pregnancy that I did when I first come home from the hospital. It is in my genes. My dad's side. I could not have made it without Chuck. I am told that I treat him mean. I guess I should be nicer. I love him, and he treats me really good. I couldn't have made it without Chuck. He says I could have and I'm sure I could have but it would have been a lot harder. I love him so much. About one year before my accident, he bought me a house. I love it. It's on a half-acre and has a swimming pool built in. I have a lot to do to it, so I can make it my own. Chuck doesn't understand that; I'm going to remodel any house we move into to make it my own. He thinks it's a waste of money because they remodeled it right before we bought it. I'm going to, I don't care.

Chapter 2: House remodel

Those of you that don't want to read the remodeling of my house turn to page 11. I would like my brother Joel to do the woodwork. He took woodshop in high school. He's very good at it. It's like he has a gift. I have my very own Clint. It can be sort of like his legacy. I can't wait to hear the ideas they have for my house. Tonja and him are very creative. First, I want a mantel over my fireplace. This house doesn't even have a mantel. Also, I would like him to build me an entertainment center and a table to go in between my chair and chucks chair. I would like a table for my fuller. I would like something by my front door. A bench with a hook above and a cubbyhole underneath to put coats and shoes. Then I want him to build me bench like seating in my kitchen. It would have storage in the bench like seating. I would have open shelving above that, and I would have me a table in front of my bench seating it would be a eat in nook. I would like my cabinets and island in a dark cherry wood color and my floors and counter tops in a lighter wood color that's like my mom's walls. It would show the darker knots and lines. I would like him to incorporate a diamond pattern in my island and my bench like seating. I would really like him to incorporate it in everything. I would like a desk bookshelves/entertainment center for my den. Last and certainly not least I would like him to build me a shed. He built himself a shed that is awesome. It has brick flooring on the outside of it. Like a big patio. He's really good at brick work too. I know he is very busy, and he is not getting any younger so maybe he can just make the plans and supervise. I have all kinds of ideas for my house. I know exactly what I want to do in my head for my house. She has a dream. A vision really. I know exactly how I want to decorate each part of my house.

I would get my niece, Joel's daughter, Naomi to paint me a mural on the wall on the lower part of the house and maybe the sky on the ceiling. I could use glow in the dark paint and everything. That would be very cool. I'd get her to do a mural in my son Joshua's room also. I would also have Joshua's name painted on his wall. It would be like calligraphy. He can have like graffiti on his wall. She (Naomi) is a very talented artist. Next, I would get my brother David to do the painting. He paints for the school board. I want my bedroom painted gray because I have two bed comforters that has the same color grey in it. The funny thing about that is I picked a comforter with Chucks favorite color in it, which is purple. He got a comforter with my favorite color, turquoise, in it. They both have the gray color in it that I want my bedroom painted in. I would like to see if I can order a set of each of them. Mine are already messing up. I would like him to paint Joshua's bedroom Jacksonville Jaguar color, teal. He got a bedroom set for Christmas. A dresser with a Jacksonville Jaguar on it and a pin board/ mirror. He also got a new jaguar bed frame; it has storage space at the bottom of the bed. The bed is full size, big enough that he has room to grow into. The other room I would like to paint it blue, for the Gators. That's going to be Chuck's office/spare room. It's going to be an office with a hideaway bed.

Chuck is an electrician. I'll get him to do all the electrical work inside and out. At least he'll draw up the plans and supervise. That sounds more like it. The next thing I would like to do is hire Rick Lenard to do a lot of stuff. He's my ex-brother-in-law. I would like him to take on a few projects. He started his own business and does repair work. First, I would get him to redo my kitchen. Right now, it's galley style. It's a little hallway. It has upper cupboards that block the view to the living room. Well, it is open from the lower cupboards to the upper cupboards, but I would like to completely open it up. I would put the open shelving where my eat in nook is going to be. I would put some wallpaper where the eat in nook is. I would also put wallpaper in the little wall going down to the lower part of the bedroom and on the sliding, doors going in the closet. I would also like some wallpaper in the hall bathroom. If I can find some that's not too busy and in my shell theme. Back to the kitchen, I want it to be opened to the living room. So, where the stove and upper cabinets are, I would put an island. I would like to change the layout. I want the sink on the island and the stove by the eat in nook at the end of my cabinets. It's very important for me to have a pot filler. I can't carry water from the stove to the sink. Maybe a drain station too. I want to build a small bathroom in the bedroom down in the lower part of the house. It has a step-down addition. The step-down addition has a dining room that we use as the kids' play area and another big room. It also has a closed-off bedroom. It's an add on addition all the way across the back part of the house. The other big room was a room for my pool table but since I came home from the hospital, I've used it as a therapy room. Chuck fixed it all up for me. He built me a big mat that has legs on it, sort of like a bed with legs and he bought me a treadmill for Christmas the year before last. I have a harness and everything. It has safety bars down one side of the room. It also has another room that is closed off. I would like to build a bathroom from the doorway over. I would like to have concrete countertops with teal paint on them. It has a door going out to the pool. That would actually bring the property value up, Chuck! I would take down that little wall on the other part of the doorway and make it one big room. I don't know about that bedroom getting cut out. It is going from a 4 bedroom to a 3 bedroom, that might lower the property value. But that is the way I want it. Maybe we could pay someone to put it back up if we ever sold the place.

I would like to decorate the lower part of the house in teal for the Jacksonville Jaguars. I would put my couch down there with a black futon bed. I would love a chase for a reading nook. Where the closet is, I would like to make Joshua a little homework area. I would put a board across it to make a table and shelves on the side. I would make it real cute for him. I shouldn't call it cute. He won't use it. I'll make it cool. I'd like some work done in my bedroom. I want double doors going out back. I won't get into what I want to do to the yard right now. I also want to redo my bathroom in the master bath. I would like to put a regular size Jacuzzi tub. And I'll take the wall out, that is where the toilet and the bathtub is. And put heated floor tiles. And I want to build a closet down in the lower part of my bedroom. Kick Chuck out of my big walk-in closet. I have dead space behind my closet where I can make my closet bigger. I feel a girl can't have a closet that is too big. I would like to have a wall with chip lap. It would be painted the same color grey. I can't really have two feature walls and I would rather have a chip-lap wall then a wall of wallpaper and I would have wallpaper on the sliding doors in the lower part of my room where Chucks closet is anyway. I know I can put wallpaper where the double doors are in the lower part of the room. Technically, that is a separate room (kind of). Oh, who am I kidding, I just want more wallpaper and me being a SPIA I want two feature walls in my bedroom. I would like to put an electric double-sided see-through fireplace on the chip-lap wall under where my TV goes. It would be with different color flames. I would have it in my luxurious closet too. And I got to have a coffee station. I have a little area in front of my bathroom, before the step-down addition. I would like to have a marble countertop. It would match the countertop for the bathroom sink. It would have a mini refrigerator and all. I'd like a pocket door where the beginning of the bathroom is. We could put a sliding door to save money. See I am money cautious. And I'm going to go ahead, go over the top and say put a skylight in my bathroom. That would be a job for my brother, Stephen. He is a roofer. He owned his own business before the economy went bad. I'll get him to do the roof stuff. The walkway to the pavilion and probably the shed. I know I dream big but if you're going to dream, dream big. Next, I would like to hire my ex-sister-in-law Kim to help me organize. I have a big laundry room that I want to organize and put shelves in the laundry room for another pantry and a couple of closet organizers. My pantry is little. My laundry room is very big and close to the kitchen. She would be a good organizer. I would also like my garage organized. I would like another bench with three hooks and three cubby holes by my garage door. See the laundry room has a door that goes to the garage. That way people can take their coats and shoes off as they come inside. It can be like a multipurpose room, a mud room/laundry/pantry. I would hire my cousin Denise to do all the sewing. She's really good at it. She sewed for Disney World one time. She still sews for a living just not for Disney World. I would get her to make me all kinds of stuff for my house. Like curtains and throw pillows, all kinds of stuff. I can't put her in here without mentioning her twin sister Jenise. She'll get mad at me. I would love to have one of them smart homes, but I got to be realistic I'll never be able to afford one of those. But I can always dream. Like I say, if you're going to dream, dream big.

There's a lot I would like to do outside. I want an awesome outside retreat all year long. First, I would like a line of tulips in between my yard and the neighbor's yard in the front on both sides. Then, I would like to fix my walk-up area to my front door. There's a garden that has a lot of rocks and a rose bush in it. It looks pretty crappy now. I haven't been able to do anything about it since my accident and Chuck don't have time. That's where a landscaper would come in real handy. He just keeps it sprayed down with weed killer. It's right by my front door. Well, there is a little concrete area too. I would like to put a little table with two chairs on it. Even if I have to put down some pavers. I would like to put something I seen on HGTV, Flip Flop. Since my accident I've been obsessed with that channel. I keep hoping I'll win a makeover 25 grand in your hand would be perfect, but I checked they don't have a comment section. If I can find one with a comment section maybe, I'll write about my story, and they'll feel sorry for me. I like the property brothers. Chuck picks on me and says that's why I like that channel. That's so untrue. I actually think Scott from Income Properties is cuter. He's just not on TV as much. He just has a baby face. Not saying there's anything wrong with the way the Property Brothers look.

Joshua wants a Ninja Warrior practice gym in the back yard. He loves that show. He also loves the show "Paradise Run". He also wants a rock-climbing wall in the back yard. He's like me, he wants a lot. I really love the Ellen DeGeneres show. She is hilarious! I would really love to meet her. I saw the first episode of her HGTV show yesterday. I was disappointed. Ellan wasn't even on it. She was on like a video chat. I did kind of like the furniture competition. Maybe she has a prior arrangement and just can't make it. I do like her talk show better anyway. I also like the show "Fixer upper" with JoeAnn and Chip Gains. They are funny. They make that show entertaining. I also like Nicole Curtis. She was right when she said she likes to be the dirtiest person on the job. She works hard. I can only watch HGTV in the morning. Chuck takes over the remote when he gets home from work sadly that's when you got to watch it to win. Chuck says that show (HDTV)is the devil and so is Pinterest. I would just like to tell everyone and chuck I come up with most of the ideas for my house remodel. Back before Sue took over my wedding. She saved me. I had a craft day planned out and everything. I was DYI crazy. Back to my story, it is a waterfall wall with fire across it. It was a really nice outdoor feature. On the back of the fire wall, I would like to put a sign that my niece Naomi made for my wedding. It says, "Chuck & Wendy's love story". On the front of the house, I have gardenia bushes. I like gardenia bushes. Mary, my old boss, loved them. She cut and grew them all over their yard. Then on the side of the house I want azalea bushes and maybe some tulips. Then I would like to put a concrete slab in the back yard, it is a wooden deck now with like a pavilion on it. I would also like an outdoor kitchen. I would also have a big screen T V, so we can watch TV and movies from the pool. It's right by my pool. I wish my pool had a heater. I'm a Floridian. I want to swim all year round. I also want a cover for my swimming pool, so the grandkids can't fall in. One that's simple to put on. I would like a slide in my swimming pool also. That would be cool. I also would like to convert my pool over to a saltwater pool. I heard there a lot easier to take care of. I would put flag tiles at the top of my pool. I would like a little area where you sit, even layout and still be in the water. I would have decorated the outside area in red, white and blue. There would be one big flag tile in the middle of the concrete area. I would also have two picnic tables. One big one for adults and one for the kids. The one I had seen on the Fixer Upper show. The tree house edition. With the Alamo wall, it would be red, white, and blue. There would be a gas fire wall, I would like to put it by my pool. Behind my pool on the other side of the yard behind the swimming pool is a big tree that I would like Joel and my dad and Joshua to build a treehouse in. Well Chuck and all my brothers actually. I would like to put a zip line from the tree house to the playhouse, but Chuck says I can't that there is no room to stop. I guess I need to have SMART goals, Specific, Measurable, Achievable, Realistic, Timely. Since he can't have that he can have an underground trampoline. I will try to put a zip line in. No promises, I will check it out and see. If I can he will have both. I would like a woodworking shed, in the back-left corner of the yard. That way we could make all kinds of stuff out of wood. That would be my she shed. I would have a pottery station. Now I'm just dreaming. You can't say I don't dream big.

On the other side of the back yard. Coming out of the double doors of my bedroom I would like a screen in the porch. To the right is my two-story playhouse. I would like to put a hot tub in the front of that. That's where a Thermal Spa would be very nice. And that shed and the covered car port I wanted is going to be in front of the hot tub. Chuck and his dad used to make leather things. He has an old belt he made. I would like to have a leather shop in the shed. I would like a basketball goal there too. I would like a concrete slab for the road, so we can keep our boat and RV. Like I said, if you're going to dream, dream big! My sister-in-law Sue ruin my dream of a circular driveway. I have a septic tank buried in the front yard. I can't put a circular driveway over a septic tank. Got to be realistic. Maybe I can move the circular driveway up a little. I want double doors where the double windows are in my bedroom. When you walk out the double doors of my bedroom, I will have a screen in the porch, to the right is the hot tub. Behind that is the two-story playhouse. I would like a wooden swing set behind the two-story playhouse, for the grandkids. Let me tell you the kids that lived here before us had it made. They had an air conditioner and cable hooked up in the playhouse and everything. Well, I want to hook it all back up. I need a fence in my backyard. Right now, we have an old wooden fence that is falling down. So, we need a new fence too. I know what I want to do in my head, but I have no idea how to put it all together. I need to hire someone to put it all together. I plan to pay for all this by writing this book. That is something I can and will do. The HDTV thing is a maybe. A large gift certificate to Wayfair would be nice. What's a nice house without nice new furniture? Our beds are past the time limit. I would like a Temperpedic and Joshua wants a sleep number. A large gift certificate to home depo would come in very handy. That's where I saw the regular size jacuzzi tub. I'd give half of the money I earned from my book to charity. The Brain and Spinal Cord Foundation and Brooks. They have done so much to help me it's unreal. It's the least I could do. Chuck has this idea of selling this house and buying a condo when Joshua moves out. Will we love it or list it? We'll see. I don't know about Chuck, but this is my forever home. Remember our motto "happy wife, happy life".

Chapter 3: My accident & my college

I was doing my clinical at Brooks one day and I wake up and I'm being sent there as a patient. I got my AA in college and was doing the LPN program when I got in my car accident. I was in the bridge program (LPN, RN). I got an Academic achievement award (that's when you make straight A's) when I got out of the hospital. I only went three terms out of four. So, close. Oh well everything happens for a reason. I'm not that smart. Chuck said I spent way too much time getting them A's. I did really bad in regular school. That's why I got a G E D instead of a high school diploma. That and I was too interested in boys. Now I would like to be a physical therapist after I finish therapy myself. Maybe work at Brooks rehab. Well, that's a long-term goal anyway. Half the battle is trying; I'll be halfway there. That I will accomplish. Yee have little faith! I can do all this; I know I can. Just like writing this book, I'm doing it! Chuck proposed to me the very first year after we bought this house. Of course, I said yes. He proposed in front of my family on Christmas day, and I loved him. He went through the proper channels and asked my dad first and everything. Then I got in my car accident. My goal was to walk down the aisle and I did. We got married October 4th, that way Chuck couldn't forget. 10, 4 good buddy. It was beautiful! Sue and Tawny did an awesome job. And I would like to take a minute to thank all my brothers and sister-in-law for helping make my day special.

There I go again, get back to the story, Wendy. I tend to get off track. I want to apologize to everyone for me bouncing from subject to subject, that's just how my brain works now. Now you are in the mind of someone with TBI. That was good I don't care who you are. "Larry the cable guy, Daniel Lawrence Whitney" says that. I like him he's hilarious. For those of you who don't quite understand, I'll put a slash in between each changed subject, and for the audio the word slash will be said. I know my book is a little unorthodox but I'm all about being different. I would really like to meet him (Daniel Whitney) and Steve Harvey too. I was just watching a video of Steve Harvey giving his audience a speech on jumping. If you don't jump, you'll never know if you can fly. Well Steve, I'm about to jump. / Àgghh(I do that a lot) Chuck is making me so mad! He is being a BAH (big A hole). My nickname for him is BAH and mine is SPIA (spoilt pain in the A). I have to admit I am. You can't fence this in, it's like holding back the wind. I love that song by Keith Urban. Sorry Lisa, maybe I'm not as cool as you think or maybe your and my idea of cool is different things. My kids are the only reason I even knew that song. I used to listen to hip hop well 95 and 97.9. Having a little beat is good when you want to dance. I used to listen to a lot of hard rock too. For some reason, the older I get the more I like country. I guess I'm getting old. Idk. Call me old fashioned but I really love old church hymns. I remember going on long road trips on vacation with my dad, I insisted on having headphones because dad always played old country or church music. I used to hate it; I thought it was torture. Now, I love it. I guess I'm getting old. Now, I like K-Love radio, they play really good music. / Chuck is making me so mad. Chuck is saying I'm not doing therapy/exercise. Well, I am. He can kiss my butt or gluteus maximious, my butt muscle. I do my therapy. Put the cameras back up then. I had so many different people at my house at first that Chuck put up the cameras. I made me a schedule and I will do it for the most part. I have been slacking on my chores. He said I don't do my occupational therapy. He doesn't realize that doing my chores and getting a bath is occupational therapy! Maybe I should be writing more, I do have messy handwriting. I used to write in my journal every day. I don't now that I'm writing a book, I'm on my tablet. Now that the dining room is clean, I can do all the things that I got my dad to build. I got him to build me all kinds of stuff I seen at Brooks. I couldn't get to them, Chuck! I couldn't go down there. It was like a big storage unit. Nickelodeon has a thing where each person went around saying I believe, and each says something different. Well, I believe I can be a great Author, and I can finish college and it's still up in the air whether I can be a physical therapist or pharmaceutical rep.

Chapter 4: My kids and Grand kids

My children made my first marriage worth it. First there is Ray. He hasn't blessed us with grandkids yet but it's best to wait until he's ready. Then there's my daughter, Ashley gave me two grandchildren. First there's Aubriella. That shows you God knows what you need. I needed that little girl. She's three and cute. I love her. When I first got home from the hospital, all I remember is I was stuck on the floor, and I was content as could be because I had Aubreilla to play with. She's not hers. Even though she looks just like her. Oh, well I love her, and she is super cute. She calls her mommy. And she gave me little Jimmie, he's 4 months. He's so adorable. He's always smiling and laughing. What can I say I love my grandkids, there the joy of my life! I didn't know grandkids could be so much fun! You can spoil them and send them home. Aaugg He's saying that half of book is what I want to do to this house, and nobody wants to read a book on how I want to remodel this house. He is being a BAH for real. That's even what he gets paid to do. They send all the people they want fired to Chuck. He says he does it for me. Don't blame me. Try and make me feel bad. You chose your profession before you even met me. Back to my story, Wendy. It's an autobiography. It's about what I like, Chuck! So, leave me alone and let me write it. If he would not have lost his notes from the hospital and all my journals I could write about other stuff, Chuck. Well, they say lashing out at people is part of my TBI so let's blame it on that (I have TBI). I use that a lot. It was true when I told that to the speech therapist. She kept saying tuck your chin before you swallow. I would tell her I forgot; I have TBI. Well, it was true I would forget. And I use "I am handicapped" as an excuse a lot too.

Chapter 5: I'm overweight.

Every time Chuck says something about my house I'm going to go back and put something else in my remodeling section. So, you can thank Chuck for the extra-long section of remodeling my house. / Opra Winfree has this saying 2016, I'm going to have the best body of my life. Well now I'm saying it. 2016 I am going to have the best body of my life. I hope to meet her one day. She's always so kind and helpful. / Kate Hutson has some new workout outfits. I would like to have some. My mom will be glad to know she is bringing back the high waisted leggings. Who wants to look at someone's butt-crack when their working out? I am very sorry to say my butt crack shows a lot. I have to say old people are very wise. I'm not used to wearing anything but low waisted pants. High waisted pants just feel weird. They hold in your stomach and hide your butt-crack. They also use them things that hold your glasses. So, you don't miss place them. They just hang on your neck, like a necklace. They even have them with jewels on them, so you can match your outfit. Red, don't you call me a wise old lady! \ I know I'm lucky to have Chuck, he has done a lot for me, and I don't know of anyone that would have done what he has done for me. He makes me so mad. I really made him mad this morning. I still am mad and it's on into the next day. He's tired of me saying and complaining that I am overweight. I came home from the hospital, and I went from a size 10 and got up to a size 16. I lost a lot of weight. I have to admit that I have been doing a lot of sit-ups and you can't even tell. I do 400 sit ups a day. Well, I just increased it was 200 and I upped it from 200 to 400. My goal is to keep my bust and lose my stomach. Every time I lose weight the first thing to go is my bust so since my stomach is the only thing, I have a problem with I thought I could just do sit ups and turn my fat stomach to flat stomach. How long does it take anyway? I've been doing it a while I should be flat. Well, I feel really tight so maybe if I continue by time summer gets here, I'll be flat. Really, I'm so forgetful I do reps of 50 at a time. Sometimes I forget what number I am on. I always try to do more. I'm not really fat. Just plump around the middle. I'm not worried, I got my dad's genes when it comes to that, and I'm determined. Someone at Planet Fitness said how determined I was. I got it from my dad. Some people call it stubbornness, but I call it determination. / I get so mad when I scare everyone from getting up from the couch and I fall back on the couch. That's where some slipper socks would be nice.

Ugh Zoie is a stupid dog, she'll bark at the back door for someone to let her out and I'll get up to let her out, walk to the back door (which is not an easy task) and she'll change her mind. Stupid dog! / I just want to say strong women survive no matter what. And what don't kill you only makes you stronger. I put that in for a friend that might need an encouraging word. By the time she reads this she'll probably be done with her ordeal, but I decided to put it in anyway. Chuck says I'm a little OCD since my accident. I'm not! Although, I have been known to do some OCD things. I do everything the same every time. Like when I take a shower, I'll shampoo then conditioner, then I brush my teeth then wash. I dry off and get out and dry again. Then I sit on the toilet and brush my hair, put deodorant on and get dressed. Then I will go put stuff in my hair. I do it the same every time because I don't want to forget, not because I'm OCD. I do think it's a little OCD when I know exactly how many squirts of bathing supplies to use. It keeps me from wasting. I don't think that qualifies as OCD. / I really hate when I think of something to write about, and I grab my phone and just that fast I'll forget what I wanted to write about. / You got to love them grand babies. Aubriella came over today, so I got my daughter to run me to the store and I bought bakery cookies, Little Debbie butterfly cakes and Easter brownies. Then they leave. She didn't eat one of them. Dieting sucks. I'm used to getting want I want when I want it. Here I am on my mat doing my exercises and what am I thinking about Bakery cookies, Little Debbie cakes and brownies. I'm pathetic. Here I am blaming little Aubriella. I should be ashamed. (Smh) / Chuck don't believe that I can do all the remodeling. It's really insulting that my own man doesn't even know me better than that! / You got to know your limitations. There's a machine at Planet Fitness and I really want to do it, but I don't do it. It is supposed to tighten up your gluteus maximus. Your butt muscles but it's kind of scary so I don't do it.

Chapter 6: friends

Well, I found out that friends are few and far between. I had a lot of friends. Now I found out who my real friends are. I have only a few now. There's Miranda. She's probably my closest friend. I hope we stay friends for a long time and grow old together. I had a good time with her tonight. She played dress up and I was the doll. That's okay. I don't stay sick long. You can play dress up with me anytime. Saves me money. Then there's Dana. She is the one that's into fitness. But IDK Miranda is getting kind of ripped. That boot camp thing has got your leg muscles defined. I saw where you do the plank on Face book. That's the hardest thing I had to do at therapy. But Dana owned a gym. She was the instructor of the spin class I went to. She lives next door. Chuck noticed Brian when we moved in, he worked with him or something. We've been good friends since day one of moving in. I'm kind of closer to her than Miranda. I've known Miranda longer, but I spend more time with Dana. Time will tell. I keep wondering if one of us move will we still be friends. I think we will. She seems like the type of person that stays your friend through thick and thin. I think that's because of her super sweet friend Kelly. They have been friends since they were like five. She spotted a good friend, and she kept her. Then there's Cliff. Him and Miranda were married when I first met them. They divorced, but they are both my friends now. Miranda is with Mike now with a new kid that's 2 years old. Cliff is married to Michelle and she's pregnant. Personally, I'm glad Cliff met Michelle; he deserves to be happy. Miranda and Cliff had Caleb. Him and Joshua are good friends. Then there's Donald and Mike. We go on the boat with Donald. I am glad Donald has Stephanie. Everyone deserves to be happy. I used to wakeboard but now I am lucky I can even get on a boat. I have gone on an inner tube. Maybe knee boarding next, then wake board. I have never been knee-boarding. Then there's Mike, we call him Mexican Mike even though he has no Mexican in him at all. Actually, I think he has African American in him. I'm not prejudiced, I have a black dog. Yeah Dana, I stole it, she said that one day. Zoie is actually white. Then there's Chris. I don't get to see him much, but I know if I need him, he's always there. Last and certainly not least there is my cousin Michelle. We will go to lunch and maybe shopping. I love shopping. She's a little down in the dumps since Aunt Pat died. I'm worried about her and I worry about her younger brother Jamie too.

Chapter 7: The hidden disability

They say TBI is a hidden disability, well unfortunately it's very visible on me. Probably from all my other injuries. I broke lord only knows how many bones. I have this thing called dystonia. It is an involuntary muscle contraction that causes repetitive or twisting movement. / I have like a little shake or jerk. I use a cup with a lid, so I don't spill all the time and I still spill the stupid drink. I am most definitely the messiest person I've ever met. Well, there's one person at Brooks Clubhouse that was messier than me. I make a mess everywhere I go. I have a speech problem too, where I had a trek. That probably bothers me more than anything else. People couldn't understand me. I was on life support a long time and I have a scar on my throat. That's probably why I have a problem with my speech and had to thicken my liquids for so long. I'm glad I don't have to do that anymore. It tasted nasty. That's probably why I cough all the time. People around me a lot just got used to it. I have a saying if I'm coughing, I'm breathing. I use a walker. I got a scar on my right ankle that goes all the way around. Where my foot was almost torn off. That's why I need a walker still. They say you learn more in the first year and I was completely non-weight bearing in the first year. I had to learn everything all over again, and I do mean everything. Shans did an excellent job putting me all back together again. I kind of feel like humpty dumpty. Well, they say your scars don't tell you where you're going just where you've been. And I'm telling you the "new me" is going to be a better me. For lunch, sometimes I'll get someone to open a can of tuna fish, I'll make tuna fish crackers. You should see me trying to open a pack of crackers I takes such a long time. And they get all squished! Every little thing takes such a big effort. You can forget me opening a can, it's impossible. It's terrible! It takes me forever to do anything. A simple task such as brushing my teeth is a big deal. It's possible for me to fix something to eat but man everything is a challenge. And to eat, I have a little shake, dystonia, so I'm kind of messy. It really makes me mad when I have to go thirsty all day because I can't grip my cup tight enough for me to open it. I put the lid on, so it can't be that tight. Well, I can always put a little tap water in a regular glass. My coordination is off. I have ataxia. That's where you lose muscle control from nonuse, sort of like deteriorating muscles. I can't move like regular people. My life sucks but the alternative is unacceptable. I miss the old me. I used to be cool, and I used to love to dance. I couldn't dance now if I tried. I could move my hips, but I can't do the feet movement. I don't care what you say being handicapped is not cool. Chucks got a cold. I guess that's my fault too. Thanks Miranda.

I'm glad my friend, Miranda is smarter than the people at the Verizon store. I went to the Verizon store; I told them my book was on the google save thing then my tablet broke for good. They couldn't find my book on google save thing. I still don't have my book. But Miranda found it once she can find it again. As long as I got my new tablet, I downloaded this notebook app, from play store. Man, I love that app. I also love Google and Bluetooth. I have to admit I have it pretty good. I do my reps on my mat, and I play on my high-tech phone playing games in between my reps and listening to music with my Bluetooth speaker. Bluetooth, I love. It is awesome. Poor Chuck he takes all the complaining about me losing my book. I got my new tablet. My old one had a foreign language written across the top and it went blank, IDK. Don't we live in America. I've had a hard time with this book. Everything's going wrong. Thank God Miranda found it! / Ugh I drop everything, and I sound so stupid, I'm just having one of them feel sorry for yourself moments. You can't even understand me. I have a bad habit of rubbing my knee, like it's hurting or something. It used to hurt, but it doesn't anymore. Maybe it's a sign of healing. IDK. / Milkshakes are my downfall! Every time I get something from a fast-food place, I get a milkshake. I go on a diet, and I'll do good for a couple of days. Then I'll buy some bakery cookies. Before the accident, I didn't even like sweets. I do now. I am terrible.

Yesterday was Chuck's birthday. I'm in the doghouse, I forgot. And my TBI excuse won't work. Ray Ray's birthday was last week. I didn't forget that. I put up reminders for him but not Chuck. I can kind of understand why he's mad. I don't know what I would do if it wasn't for Chuck, he does everything for me. I knew he wouldn't remind me about Ray Ray. I thought he would remind me about his birthday. But noooooo! Mike and Red and Ashley come over with the grandkids for his birthday. / Well, I got some good news; I'm going to have a granddaughter named Riley. I'm not sure if that is the way Ashley is going to spell her name but that's what they're naming her. I can't wait to buy little girl clothes. Aubriella was two when I met her. I didn't get to buy baby girl clothes. It's perfect Ashley has a boy and now she's going to have a girl. Really two girls counting Aubriella. / We went to Cliff and Michelle's yesterday. It was nice. I haven't seen them in a while. Michelle says you have got to lose weight. If I don't then my fat will just turn into muscle. That would be gross. I would have one big ball of muscle on my stomach. / Well Dana confirmed I have to lose weight to get rid of my stomach. That fat would turn into a big ball of muscle. Ewww, that would be nasty. Guess I need to go on a diet. It seems I'm doing all these sit ups for nothing.

Chapter 8: fathers and Valentine's day

Well, it's Father's Day and I let Chuck sleep in till after 11. Then I go to fix him some breakfast. The first time I cook since my accident. I made scrambled eggs with cheese and some instant cheese grits. He informs me very rudely that he doesn't like instant grits. What an inappreciable BAH / I just got to tell the people that have insomnia that it really is a terrible thing. I never had insomnia before my accident. I remember going to night school and I could bring a little sandwich for lunch, and I could go to my car and gobble it down and I could take a nap the rest of the time. I could fall asleep on a dime. Now I take a prescription of Tramazapam for bedtime and take an over the counter sleeping pill for when I wake up to use the bathroom at 1 through 5 AM. If I don't have them, I'll just watch the time fly by. I have one of them alarm L E D clocks that shows what time it is. I'll lay there and watch the minutes pass.1,2,3,4,5.... It's awful. Tick tock, tick tock. I don't hear that, but I might as well. It's kind of odd that I damaged the occipital lobe that controls your consciousness, and they thought I would never wake up, now I can't sleep. / I think that if I didn't have TBI I would have never been able to write a book. I would have just been sad. Well, an autobiography anyway. Now if I was beaten and abused or if I was drinking and driving. If I have something I overcame.

I can't believe it. It is Valentine's Day and Red ask Ashley to marry him. About time Red. Two kids later. I'm happy for both of you. I realize it's hard to make that big of a decision. I like giving him a hard time. It's just what we do. / Well, I got a pretty good valentine's day present. I'm lucky I got what I got. Forgetting Chuck's birthday and all. I got some candy and a real pretty rose bush, it's little now in a metal container, it has flowers all over it and I can plant it in my walkway garden. My first thing to my design. If I don't kill it. I'm terrible with plants, that's why I want annuals for my yard. I want a whole bunch of tulips. I really like them. My mom has a line of them by her fence. I can just get me a sprinkler system that I set to go off every day and keep them weeded out. That's where a landscaper would be very nice. / My speech therapist, Ceil, said I can make my voice stronger if I sing in church. So, I sing in church and in Sunday school but not during invitation. I don't want to scare anyone. That would be terrible. Scare someone with my stupid sounding voice while they are being convicted by God.

Awe man I forgot to water the plants. Oh well, an extra chore for tomorrow. / Verizon redeemed themselves. The guy there said I looked like I had joy bursting from me when I walked in the door. He nicknamed me glory giver. It's like we had revival right in the store. It was great. Sometimes it's not the establishment, it's all according to who you get. Not that the first visit was bad, it was just not very productive. / I just seen this commercial, and this lady was texting and her whole family got in a car accident. Do NOT text and drive. Look at me. I'm so glad nobody was with me when I got in my accident. I don't think I could live with myself if I hurt or kill someone especially a loved one. That would be terrible. I just got to say that I wasn't ever a good driver. You can ask all my kids and my ex and my husband or anyone that's ever rid with me. They'll all tell you I can't drive. I need a driver. I've hit more than one parked car. Who hits a parked car? There's your sign. I have figured out I'm better off not driving! I heard the guy that was driving the semi-truck never drove a semi again. I just wanted to tell him that it's not his fault, I was the one texting. I really feel bad. That was his lively hood. I feel awful. But I would have never become an Author. Everything happens for a reason. / I want to tell you something I feel very guilty about. I was at church, and I saw a guy I grew up with. Sporadically, I gave him a big hug. I don't think Chuck would understand and by the look on his mother's face it was inappropriate. I wasn't even thinking about it, it just happened. I do care about him I've known him all my life. I don't want anyone to take what I did the wrong way. I love Chuck, I would never do anything to mess it up. He'll read this sooner or later. I don't want anything in our relationship a secret. I found out later that he probably needed that hug. God works in mysterious ways.

Chapter 9: Little Dave died

12/12/89 - 2/14/15

r.i.p lil dave

I got some terrible, terrible news my brother David's oldest son little Dave died. I can't believe it. I'll never see him again. He (little Dave) was so cute when he was little. He had long blond hair and blue eyes. I can't believe I'll never see him again. Not in this lifetime anyway Well we went to see David today. I don't know what I would do if one of my children died. It's just not natural. You're supposed to die before your kids. I know I'll dedicate this book to little Dave. Well, we're hopefully going to go to lunch with Sharon and momma Gene real soon. Sharon is Little Dave's mom and momma Gene is his grandma. I have no coffee creamer. I'm so neglected and mistreated. I guess not having coffee creamer one day wouldn't make me mistreated and neglected it just sucks. Man, I lost my book. It disappeared off my tablet. I think I sent it to Chuck; he hasn't looked yet. I'll give him one more day before I go off on him. I've been patient long enough. I think my book is more important to me than anyone else. Sometimes you just got to go off. Chuck doesn't have it. Well, I sent it to Dana, but I added it after that. Well at least I'll have most of it. My bad memory I don't think I'll remember it. My brother Paul is here, with his daughter Holly and her daughter Bailey. Actually, I have pictures with Bailey from when they come to see me in the hospital. I don't remember seeing Bailey, but oh well. I couldn't lie about seeing stuff when I was in the hospital. Some people say they seen Jesus or passed away relatives, the pearly gates, something but not me. Not saying that people are lying. What do I know, I have a traumatic brain injury? I don't remember anything from when I was in Acoma. I believe anything is possible through God. Paul, Holly, Bailey, Jennelle, and little Shelby came by to see me. It was good to see them. It's a shame someone has to die to get to see everyone. I actually am kind of excited about little Dave's funeral, as shameful as it sounds. I'm going to get to see people I haven't seen since way before my accident. / Paul you'd better be glad you live in New Mexico. I'd put your butt to work doing something on my home design. / It's president's day. Joshua didn't have to go to school today and I took a Temazepam (a prescription sleeping pill) to help me sleep in. I was almost a nurse; I know what I'm doing. I won't do that again. I was a little dizzy this morning. / I'm going to be so mad if I can't cry at little Dave's funeral. I damaged the occipital lobe. It controls your emotions. I was so mad at Pat's funeral, I couldn't cry. She was my favorite Aunt. I felt like crying, I just couldn't. I used to cry even if I didn't like the person. I'd cry because the loved ones were crying. Back to my story, Wendy. I hate it when I do that. That's the very back part of your brain, your occipital lobe. Something I had seen on Facebook said it controls your emotions. I googled it and all I see it keeps saying that it controls your vision. That would explain why I think things seem closer than they are. When I'm trying to walk, I'll reach for something, and I can't reach it. My perception is off. I had double vision at first and my vision is blurry sometimes. But I couldn't find anything else, especially on emotion. I just wanted to say thank you mom and dad. I don't know what I would have done if it wasn't for my family. My mom and dad, Ashley and Chuck and Joshua and Ray all do a lot to help me. Even Red does a lot for me. I feel very fortunate.

I can't believe it, Aunt Ann passed away. Two viewings in one week, that's terrible! She's Chuck's Aunt. She made me feel like I was part of the family. There's a saying out there that death comes in three, so I guess I'll see who goes next. I went to three funerals last time. It was since my accident. It was Aunt Pat, Scott, and Barbara. There's a fourth person, Bro. Henry, but Chuck wouldn't let me go to the funeral. I wasn't very close to him anyway. Chuck thought it would make me depressed. You know I'm really glad I don't have to deal with that. I would hate to be depressed all the time. I honestly don't think you will go to hell if you kill yourself if you are depressed. Depression is a sickness. God isn't going to through you in hell if you are sick. My God is a merciful God. Gods' mercy is what we need most. He has been very merciful to me. I should be dead. I shouldn't be able to earn a living. Be able to even walk. He isn't going to throw you in hell because you are sick. Plus, John 3:16. All you have to do is believe in him and you will not perish but have ever lasting life. I don't know why I brought that up, trust me it isn't that bad. That reminds me of a country song I like "John3:16" by Keith Urban.

It's been two weeks since I started exercising my arm again and it still hurts. I wonder how long it takes anyway. I can't believe I have arthritis. / I just beat my daughter Ashley at Trivia Crack. I posted on Facebook. "How does it feel to get beat by a handicap that has TBI." Hehe bahhaha. / Well Aunt Anne's funeral was today. I know I'll see her again one day. I didn't get to go to the funeral. Chuck was in a rush with work and all. But he did come and get me to go eat afterwards with the family. He is close to Aunt Ann's son, Gary. They were like really good friends growing up. Sharon, David's ex-wife stopped by today. I really like her. She's always a lot of fun to be around. / Chuck came home from work, and I have been gone about 30 minutes or so and he calls me up saying Zoie is upside down in the garbage can. That stupid dog. I have a garbage can at the end of the couch, so I can put my trash in, Zoie got up on the couch and in the garbage, she went. Guess I need to put the lid on it. Quitters never win or prosper. So, I'm not going to quit my book. I'm going to give Chuck till Monday before I say anything. It's Friday now. I'm not going to complain too much. Chucks been working such long hours. I'm going to put it on Facebook. Maybe one of my Facebook friends is computer savvy and can help. The problem is it is on a notebook, tablet thing not a computer. / I sent Ashley a message in trivia crack, "can't believe you would beat a handicap and that has a traumatic brain injury. I better watch out she won't play me. / I have to admit, I cheat at four pictures one word. I downloaded the cheat app for it. Well, I just don't understand, why is that worse than sending it to everyone so they can tell me the answer. / Well, I went to my eye doctor's appointment. I'm proud to say I am 20\20. Well, I'm still wearing my reading glasses to use my phone or notebook. It's a strain to see when I don't wear them. Do they give you prescription glasses if all you need is over-the-counter glasses? I guess the doctors can't prevent you from getting old. But if you got to get old get old in style. On the bright side the Dollar Tree has reading glasses for $1. At that price I can afford a pair to go with every outfit. That's like my new thing. We went to church. We had a visitor preacher, Bro. Hayward. Right now, I'm mad at BÀH. I am saying "you can't say anything nice then don't say anything at all." I even went to church. It didn't even help. / I went to church and it's Wednesday. For one Joshua loves Patch the Pirate. Plus, it gives me encouragement in the middle of the week. My eyes are on you lord don't let me fall, show me the way. Give me the strength to get through this personal hardship I'm going through.

Chapter 10: Chuck's family

It's going to be a sad, sad day when we lose Uncle Marshal. He's like the rock that holds this family together. Hopefully we got a while though. My favorite person in Chucks family other than Tracey is Amanda. She seems like a hippie chick. Really, I like everyone in his family, but I really like Amanda and Tracey. Tracey is more like his sister than his cousin. Now she is like my sister. I like all Tracey's kids, but I really like Miranda. She's a single mom of four girls. She is a good mom too. Miranda has a good career, and all her kids are so respectful. / I wanted to say something about Cory and Renee. Renee is Dee's sister. I've known her since I was a kid. Not as good as I've gotten to know her since my accident. She's really cool and nice. Cory, I admire him. He's worked really hard and put himself through college to become a teacher. He was a lead singer and guitarist in a band before he finished college. He put together a little fundraiser for me. I think Renee did a lot with that too. She helps people in need. Him and his band did the fundraiser. They are both (Cory and Renee) special to me. Like extended family, their mom and dad too. / Jimmie, he is so funny. He was walking with my walker, and I was with him, well my dad come over to take Joshua to swim meet. Anyway, he stopped and looked up at him and let go and fell straight on his head. Now every time he looks at me, he whines. It's been like 2 hours. It hurt his feelings that I let him fall. Poor thing he's broken hearted.

Oh, Chuck, so sweet. He's taking me to Fernandina Beach on Friday after work. I'm so happy and excited! I can't believe it. We're going to do something at two o'clock. I can't wait! Hopefully we'll have lots of fun.

We got a beach view hotel and everything. / Oh yeah, Mike and I were talking about careers and our future. Well after Chuck burst my bubble in the pharmaceutical rep thing. He said that pharmaceutical reps have to travel. Mike said I can run from my home a physical therapy for the handicap. This one guy says he is a physical therapist from his home because influenced by his physical therapist that he became one himself, sort of like me and Lisa, my physical therapist. I remember Lisa doing a lot of lifting on the patients. Maybe I can pay like my driver to do the lifting. Chachinng. I have a new plan. I'll be like the brains of the operation. "The physical therapy from home thing." I can even do water aerobics one day a week. Like Sat. That would be perfect.

I just want to say I miss me some Jimmie. It's nice to be home. Ashley came over with the kids today. I made grits and eggs for breakfast and mac-n-cheese and hotdogs for lunch. I figure I don't have a therapist anymore so I can do what I want. You hear that, Ashley Nicole. Just teasing. That is my daughter's name also. Nikki is what she (one of my new therapists) likes to be called. I've been dying to call her that since day one of knowing what her name was. I didn't want to undermine her authority. See I am nice. I used to call my daughter when she was in trouble. Yeah, I'm starting easy. You got to know your limitations. I don't carry any boiling water, just stuff like that. / We are getting together at my brother Joel's house. I can't wait. I just found out; my niece Naomi is going to backpack around Europe. I hope she has fun! I'm actually kind of envious. I went to Europe with a college class. It was definitely an experience that I'll never forget. I stayed in hotels of course. I bought a leather jacket when I was in Europe and I told this lady from church, Mrs. Dickerson. She told me the next time someone says something about my leather jacket I should tell them it's real Italian leather. I bought it when I was in Italy. She told me to say it really snobbish like. Well, I did and to my embarrassment it was my former pastor of our church, Dr. David Strunk. I couldn't have been more embarrassed. I'm so proud of her (Naomi). She got some money when she turned 18 and she bought herself a house. I couldn't be prouder. She's going to Holland with her mom Tonja, to visit with her mom and grandma for two weeks, then off she goes, touring Europe. I'm so jealous. A little scared but more jealous.

Chapter 11: Ashley's baby shower

Once again Chuck thinks too much of himself, I went to mom's house last night the family was getting together to have chili at moms and I told Chuck I would bring him home some chili, he had to work. I said something about it to mom and then fell asleep. So sorry I didn't wake up thinking about your chili. / Ashley and Kaitlyn (Tommy's youngest girl) came over with all the kids to plan Ashley's baby shower. It's my last chance to get it right. The last one sucked. It didn't even have any games. Anyway, I love kids but 5 of them together can be a little much. They left the house clean, and I didn't have to hear Chuck complain. I have to say I enjoyed myself. / I hope Chuck knows how much I love him. I know I have it good. It's all because of you. I feel bad cause he has to take all my complaining for me losing my book. / I'm proud to say that I at least found half of my book. I figured it out all by myself. The passwords anyway, I have a bad habit of changing the password and forgetting them. Now I just need to figure out the new password on the google save thing. /I love the Shick Intamate. I can literally go sideways and not cut myself. Shawnica, (my occupational therapist), I bet I wouldn't have cut myself for that shaving test if I had that razor. I still hate shaving though. That's where laser hair removal would be real nice. IDK though, I heard it leaves bumps on a lot of people. I wonder if the bumps are permanent or temporary. Time to do some research. It's worth a try if the bumps only last a week or two. I ended up having to buy me a new razor. It's called "The Shick Intuition", the store didn't have the other one. It's Just like the other one, it's just a different color. Well last night I really had to restrain myself. I was definitely saying "Wendy be good" over and over in my head. Now I just really need to forget the whole situation. So, I'm going to change the subject to some of Facebook inspirational sayings. That might make me feel better. I really think I did good. I'm proud of myself. Here is a saying from Rockin Wellness Inc. " Not till we are lost do we find ourselves." Well, I feel like I found myself through all of this. There is one that says " I asked God why is he taking me through the water....he said because your enemies can't swim." I have to believe God has a reason for letting this happen to me. Here is one that I like. I think it's pretty inspirational. " I thank God for protecting me from what I thought I wanted and blessing me with what I didn't know I needed." Here is one from Handicap this. "Strong people don't put other people down they lift them up."

Aubriella finally got to eat a cookie. Then I ate the last brownie for lunch. I came back from the gym and then Olive Garden for lunch with Sharon and what did I do. I ate bakery cookies, Little Debbie cakes and brownies. I'm pathetic. / Poor Chuck he has worked for almost 4 weeks with no days off. He worked 3 weekends with the 5-day weekdays, so we can catch up. His work should know he's not as young as he used to be. He could have had a heart attack or something. Then what would I do. I have to say, that's just wrong, even for me. I hope he knows how much I love and appreciate him. / My son Ray came by. He commented that I wasn't doing the sit ups right. I wasn't laying all the way down, so I started to do them right and that was about a month ago. I have got about a month before I start swimming so maybe by time, I have to wear a swimsuit I'll be flat. I guess I'm going to have to go on a diet. I gained five lbs. I lost 20 lbs. and gained 5. Muscle weighs more than fat so when I lost 20lbs. I thought I was something else. I remember I fell one day. It had been a while, and I was a bit shaken up, so I rewarded myself with a milkshake. Can't do that anymore. I fell today even though I wanted to buy myself a milkshake I was good, I didn't. Aubreilla has a doctor's appointment tomorrow. She is getting shots and they are supposed to come here afterwards. So, I saw this on Facebook where you feel the popsicle makers up with gummy bears and they put sprite in it, but I took it to the next level, and I put Fanta Strawberry soda in it instead of sprite. That should make her feel better. Hope I don't eat all of these.

I called all my friends (well texted really) to say that I lost my book, and nobody cares. I knew one of them would find it. Hehe Miranda texted the next morning. / I know I went through a terrible, terrible ordeal that I wouldn't wish upon my worst enemy, but for some reason I feel very fortunate and blessed. I have a beautiful home even without my interior design and a man that has unconditional love, and a large family that loves me and has done so much to help me. I am blessed! I see how fortunate I am now. I think I took everything for granted before. / I just got to say I don't have any enemies that I know of anyway. / TBI hope and Inspiration says "Don't feel bad if people only call you when they need something. Be privileged that you are the candle that comes to their mind when they're in darkness." Someone very near and dear to me needs to hear that one. They also have one that say's "If opportunity doesn't knock build a door." I thought that one was very inspirational. / Unbelievable how a Brain damaged b**ch can write a book. As a so-called Christian told me, unbelievable. Well, I got this TBI thing. My brain works just fine. I'm smarter than most people I know. I just can't seem to get what I want to say out. And it takes a long time to think of something to say sometimes.

Chapter 12: I love my Church

I have become like best friends with my daughter and my mom. I couldn't be happier! I think Ashley is my true best friend. I couldn't ask for anything better. Miranda and Dana have their own family. They both have little ones. Everyone should know that family comes before friends. That's why being best friends with my daughter is so good. I went to Joel's for Sue's birthday! I had a lot of fun. He agreed to make my mantel. Bahaha. The master plan begins. / The plant I got for Valentine's Day died. / Red usually helps me with all my computer problems since he did go to college for computers. But since Red is one of the unfortunate guys working for Chuck out of town, I'm getting Michael Cantenberry (Tommy's oldest) to help. He's really smart. Now my book is lost in the cloud. What's that? Before I got into my accident a cloud was a big poof in the sky that sometimes holds rain. / My dad is very determined and he's like a big kid. I remember him coming over to my house first thing one morning asking me to wake the kids up to jump on the trampoline. I bought the property next door to them at that time. Back to my story Wendy. Well, I'm pretty driven. Always have been. I've always gone to school and stuff, but I think I'm more driven now than before. I'm really determined. Determined to prove everyone wrong. / My dad has this shirt he wears. He got it when he went up the stairs of the highest building in Jacksonville and it says it too. I call it his bragging shirt. / I used to be worried about college but I'm not anymore. If I can memorize 20 days of 5 words each day, then I can remember anything! That's 100words. Well, it sounded better in my head.

It's about time to go on the boat again. Between the water being too cold and Chuck having to work all the time, we hadn't gone out yet. / " À river can run through a rock not because of its strength but because of its persistence", I thought that was relevant. I always said even before the accident that I would be old and gray and still going to college. Alzheimer's disease runs in the family. They say that if you keep an active mind it helps. IDK, if it's true but it can't hurt. I'm going to do an experiment. I'm going to go take college courses probably till I die, then I'll see if that works. / I finally did exercises in the pool. I've gone swimming quite a few times, just without exercising. I just relaxed and had fun. I took a little me time. / I was so proud of my boy Joshua. He came in first twice and second once at the swim terminate. / Ashley kept going around the house complaining that she couldn't poop. Well, I followed her around the house with a bottle of stool softener. Telling her to take some, that I know someone who died from that. She made me promise, that if she ever did die from that, that I would put "that s*it finally killed her" on her tombstone. There I go again, bouncing from subject to subject. / My new shoes came in the mail today. I was hoping they would come on Red's birthday. That way I could tell him to look at the new shoes I got for your birthday. 😊 / I went to church. I went to church this morning. I have to say I had a good time. I know church is not supposed to be a social event, but it sure helps when you are around a bunch of people you enjoy being around. Sharon was there. I love her to death and she's always fun to be around. I got to see Brenda too. I didn't actually speak to her. Hi Brenda. I got to talk to Miss. Nelson too. I also seen both Tammie's. And let's not forget Kathy. Well, and all the old timers, like all the Snailgroves. The people that had been there since I was little. There like pillars, part of the foundation that makes the church.

I went to Wet-n-Wild with Joshua's swim team. I went and bought a new bathing suit. One that the top comes all the way to the bottom. Nobody wants to see a bunch of belly fat. It's kind of weird but I kind of knew I was going to get in an accident before I did. I get premonitions, I guess. I've gotten three of them so far. One, it was when I was little, I had one of my dad's car accident. I was asleep, and I woke up from a dream of my dad getting in a car accident. I went back to sleep and when I woke up dad had stitches in his chin and the car was totaled. The second one I won't mention, and the third one was my car accident. I had that one quite a few times. Also, I kind of knew where I was going to get into my accident. I was stopping at that light, and I remember thinking that if I do get in an accident, I am going to do it here. I also remember trying to stand one day and catching my footing and thinking I can't imagine not being able to walk. I thought I was crazy. At that point, it was unthinkable. / I really miss driving! I can't go anywhere! I wish I could afford to pay someone to drive me around. I also need my own vehicle. I don't want to share one with Chuck. Well maybe I can be in a Subaru commercial. " I lived, "After what I went through, I'll only drive a Subaru". I need to get one big though like a SUV or something. I need something big enough for all the grandkids. One with all the bells and whistles. I also need a trailer for my scooter and golf cart. I need a new golf cart. My other one messed up. That way I can go to the mall or the flea market or the park or something. I can't walk that far.

Chapter 13: I miss not driving

Chuck said my concentration isn't long enough to drive. He's probably right. I was driving one of them riding carts at the grocery store and I ran into the line of carts. I was looking out the window, it was raining. If we were in a car and someone would have got hurt, I would of never forgive myself. I'll be honest with you; I stole the keys to my car. I took the car one day. I only went in the neighborhood, and I went backway to the Gate Station. Well after I did that at the grocery store, I gave my keys up. It would be bad if I hurt someone else. It's bad enough for me hurting myself but I couldn't live with myself if I hurt someone else. / I'm watching flea market flip on HDTV. I love that show. I want to do that! Maybe Chuck and I against Ashley and Red. At the Waldo Flea Market or Lake City Flea Market. All the flea markets in Jacksonville are too small. I think Steve and Dee would be more competitive. IDK though, Red thinks he would be good at it. I would say Joel and Tonja, but I want competition not to lose. Oh, I can't be like that. I would be a good loser. I know the winner can buy the loser lunch or dinner. And I don't sit and watch HDTV all day! I watch it in the morning while I eat breakfast and while I eat lunch and while I rest before Joshua and Chuck get home. It is on the T.V. station during the day.

It's fun to watch your grandkids play. Papa Chuck is teaching Aubriella to play hopscotch. I wish I could play. I know I can make that to be a long-term goal to play hopscotch with Aubriella. Don't worry, I know my limitations. I made me, Jimmy, Aubriella and Joshua a milkshake. Hmmmmmm, it was good. / I have a confession. That song I downloaded "Mary did you know" by Pentonics and "This is my fight song". By Cali Bevira, a cancer survivor that was on the Ellan Degenerates show. She also got a standing ovation and the golden ticket by Simon on America has Talent show. I can't find it. Stupid smart phone or I guess it could be an operator error. Nikki, one of my therapists used to say that when I used to kick my walker. My dad calls the smart phone smarter than me phone. I guess I'm not as smart as I thought.

I also got the first sun of summer. I was wearing pants: just on my face, arms and shoulders. Yeah, they were a little burnt. Don't worry, I was tanned by morning. I would love to try spray tanning. You don't have to worry about the UV rays hurting your skin. I can tell it's going to be a fun in the sun summer. But jaws started dropping when Wendy started walking. I love that song. Well, I guess I haven't changed that much. I'm still the same Wendy. That's what makes me, me! Well, there is nothing wrong with looking your best. I was almost killed in a car accident, sent to hospice and I still got it! / Before I had Joshua, I would have never thought I would be overweight. Thanks Josh! Something about having a kid after your 30. You just don't bounce back like you did when you were in your twenties. I think I looked pretty good. I was considered to be what the kids called a M.I.L.F. If you don't know what that means I'm not going to tell you. Ask a teenager. Now since the accident I don't think I'm all that. My face is chubbier than I want, and I have a belly that I don't want. I just look kind of old. I'm 43. That's kind of old. Ask a little kid. I have grey hair. I just keep it dyed. The big thing is I'm handicap. Say what you want but a handicap is not cool. Facebook has a saying from handicap this it says, "Faith is daring your soul to go beyond what your eyes can see". / We had a big party planned for Joshua's birthday, but we all woke up sick. A stomach virus or something. Well, we ended up having to cancel it. We were going to have a paint ball party. Where all the guys and their fathers could go to play paintball. Then they could come back to the house for cake and swim. It would have been real fun. But it is what it is. Last year he had a birthday party at Rebounders. That's a place that has a whole bunch of indoor trampolines. / Joshua is a Mother's Day baby. He was born on Mother's Day. He was born around 2 o'clock in the morning so he was in my arms by 9 o'clock. It was a great Mother's Day. I named him Joshua Aaron. The two men that walked by Moses side. The funny thing about that is I didn't know that when I named him. I found that out when I told mom what his name was. / The greatest gift for a Christian mother is to know your children are saved. So, you can spend eternity with them. I am very thankful; I think all of my children are saved. / It's kind of funny but I was watching TV with Ashley and playing on my phone, and I told her I was multitasking, and she just laughed at me and said mom, you never could multitask. It just reminded me of a time at therapy and Lisa, my physical therapist, was having me to walk around the therapy room and I saw Shanika, my occupational therapist, and I started to talk to her, and she told me I need pay attention to my walking, and Lisa said something to the affect I was doing good at both, and I made a big deal about being able to multitask. Lisa, I have never been able to multitask. When I was younger, I use to walk into poles ask my cousin Michelle. Everyone I know knows I've never could multitask. / It's about time to go on the boat again. Between the water being too cold and Chuck having to work all the time we hadn't gone out yet. / I did something to Ashley, but I can't remember what. Idk, I do remember she was just being hormonal.

Well, I'm still doing 400 setups and haven't lost any weight. My stomach muscles hurt. / Aubriella and I are learning to swim together. She's a little further behind then me but still were learning together in the same summer. It's fun learning to do things with your grandkids. / We had Ashley's baby shower today. There were lots of people, nice decorations, and plenty of food. I have to say I enjoyed myself. / Ashley is all mad at me. I thought I was a good person but after reading this book and after thinking about what I say to people makes me wonder. I remember telling someone the worst thing I ever did to someone is at camp one year I was using this girl's curling iron with wet hair, and she told me that you're not supposed to use a curling iron with wet hair it might break it and I used it anyway. You know, what you say to people can be more hurtful than what you do. My daughter just told me I'm not a bad person, I'm just sassy. Well, that doesn't make me feel too bad. I'm only mean to the people I'm closest to.

mean I'm just straight up. Even though I am learning that can be hurtful sometimes. Dee asked me if I remember everything from before the accident, I said I do and for the most part I do but like my schooling I forgot most of it. Even though I couldn't tell you most of that before my accident. I guess it comes back to you when you need it, science is my best subject in Trivia Crack. I also play word crack. I have more of a short-term memory loss. Like I can't remember what just happened. I couldn't tell you what I ate for lunch last week. Or what I did earlier that day. When I first went to Brooks Clubhouse the director there asked me a medical question just to see if I remembered. She asked me what normal blood pressure was. I think I got one of the numbers right. I couldn't even tell what your blood pressure should be after my accident. I remember what it should be now.

Chapter 14: Ashley had baby Rylee

#25

Ashley had baby Rylee today. She came out little sooner than we wanted but she's healthy. That's all you can ask for. / It's July 2nd and Reds mom Laura is here. We bought a whole bunch of fireworks for the 4th, mortars and all. Our next-door neighbor Brian usually does a lot too. / Well, I haven't said much about my little grandson Jimmie. Jimmie is so cute and mischievous. Ashley says that the two words don't remotely go together. But that's my Jimmy for you. He's got a long bruise on his head from throwing himself on the floor pitching a fit. He's so cute. He may be the little, biggest brat I ever did see. He's a happy baby most of the time. LAH, that's his nickname, he'll pitch a fit like you've never seen before. Talk about brat, that he is. Aubriella never got into anything. Jimmie tries to get everything, and he gets very mad if he doesn't get it. Today Ashley is supposed to come home from the hospital. The baby is still too small, but Ashley is good to go. What can I say about my beautiful Rylee? She has the cutest chubby cheeks I ever saw, and she has the prettiest blue eyes just like her nana. She's got the prettiest face ever. / I used to go camping all the time. I used to go camping with my mom's side of the family. Eiland family camping trip. That used to be so much fun. I used to take my kids camping a lot too. I can't go now. I can't sleep in a tent on an air mattress. That's where an RV would be great. Here is a saying from Rockin Wellness Inc "Not till we are lost do we find ourselves. " Well, I feel like I found myself through all of this. There is one that says " I asked God why is he taking me thru the water....he said because your enemies can't swim." I have to believe God has a reason for letting this happen to me. Here is one that I like. I think it's pretty inspirational. " I thank God for protecting me from what I thought I wanted and blessing me with what I didn't know I needed." Here is one from Handicap This. "Strong people don't put other people down, they lift them up.

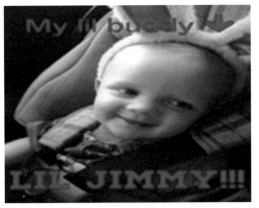

It is little Jimmies birthday party. We are doing it in mickey mouse since his favorite show is Mickey Mouse Clubhouse. We got plenty of decorations and two cakes (one for him and one for us). We got Nikki (one of Tommy's girls) to do the cake. She wanted to stay home with her kids, so she started a cake decorating business. It was a great Mickie Mouse cake. She did an excellent job. We had a pool party and everything. It was great. / They have neat sayings on the walls at Shans one said "Kindness is timeless and so easy to give. It only takes a moment to show someone that you care". I hope I got that right. I didn't write them down and I do have a traumatic Brain injury, so I may have gotten some of the words wrong on the other one later in the book as well. I bought myself a new cup. Its turquoise color and it says "Be STRONG and COURAGEOUS do not be afraid for the lord your God is with you wherever you go. Joshua 1:9 I like that, I got a new favorite cup. / I used to love to cook I think I baked better than anything else. I love Racheal Ray. I think she's awesome. I make a mean Shepard's pie (a meatloaf with mash potatoes and cheese on top). I want to be able to cook again. I hate not being able to cut things. Like cut up little pieces of chicken up for chicken and dumplings. That's where the Sammeri 360 would come in real handy. I have just a plain pizza cutter now. It's not that sharp. I can't cut up meat with it. My mom said they have what looks like a pair of scissors but they are meant to cut up meat. Everyone is scared I'm going to cut myself. They are also afraid I'm going to burn myself. I enjoy cooking so leave me alone and let me cook already. I want a food processor big enough to put whole potatoes in. I can make scalloped potatoes again. One of my friends loved my scalloped potatoes. She asks for it all the time. If I started cooking Chuck would never cook again except on his Orion grill. That you just marinade it and put it in and come back in like 3 hours and take it out. And it's oh so good. I cook in the crock pot now. I think Racheal Ray has a Crockpot Cookbook; I want one.

I like chef Ramsey too, with Hell's kitchen. I would like to eat there one day. Even if I could cook good enough to be a chef I would not want to be on his show. You're a chef because you love to cook. It's something you really enjoy doing. Who wants to be cussed out? That's not too enjoyable. / Today is Sunday and I am proud of myself. I went to church. I love my church, everyone needs the lord, I really love my, Blanding Blvd. Baptist Church. I love that song "I love my church", By Tim McGraw. Well, I think a few different people sing that song. Everyone there is like an extended family. Like (Aunt Shirly, Uncle

Bill, and Aunt Fay) they are not really family. We just call them that. Let's not forget Mrs. Waters. She's not really family either but in my heart, she is. She asked me one time am I happier now or before and if I could go back and change what happened to me would I? I told her no; I am happier now. / I am still doing all my exercises. I do all my mat exercises in the morning. After lunch I do my bar exercises. I haven't walked to Dana's or walked on the treadmill in a while. There is reasoning for me thinking the way I do about people giving up on me. But Chuck is always so tired all the time. He works all the time. I wouldn't want to deal with me after a hard day of work either. Now Laura went home. Guess I won't be going to Phenix Arizona anytime soon. Ashley was going to take me with her to Arizona. Better off anyway. Ashley would have a five-year-old, a newborn, Jimmie – which is enough all alone and me a handicap on an airplane. Red couldn't go. He had to work.

I woke up this morning with my eye all swollen and red. It was all blood shot. So, Chuck took off and took me back to Shans. I have to admit I didn't put my antibiotic drops in my eye like I should have. I found this neat saying on the cafeteria wall; I think the time before last. I thought it was inspiring. "When faced with a mountain, climb over, pass through it, or tunnel underneath it. Let self-confidence guide your actions. The greatest treasure is sometimes found in places we least expect." I thought it was inspirational. / Baby Reilly is coming home from the hospital today. She is so precious. I went to my postOp apt. and was asking the doctor about my activity level, and he told me to use common since and someone told him I didn't have common since (I guess because of my accident). Well, I got enough common since to know that's not a very nice thing to say.

Chapter 15: Aubreilla's Birthday

Aubreilla's birthday party was today. She wanted it all done up in Frozen. She had a pool party and everything. It was great! We bought her a frozen karaoke machine; we got the best present. / I sound really stupid. I was at the gym today and a man started talking to me and I tried to talk to him back and he couldn't understand me, my mom had to interpret for me. / April 3rd at 10:30pm Chuck said he was going to beat me then he said he loves me and gave me a kiss. He told me to write that. / Chuck is so funny. He said doing my chores was my job, just like I said getting Joshua off to school is my job as a mother. It's my job as a housewife. Ha, I like that. That's a good one, Chuck. /Chuck is such a good father. Chuck come out with a whole bunch of bags with a whole bunch of school supplies and his lab top and started reading off a list of supplies that Joshua needed to take for the first day of school. I'm so proud of Joshua. He's going to a magnet military program. He has uniforms now. He wanted to; he picked it out. Well, he is little for his age. But man, he is nothing but muscles. He is ripped. Joshua's always going around showing off his 6 pack. He (or we) figures it'll toughen him up some.

Well, I did it again. I said something to make Chuck mad. I can't even have his back when no one is around. Man, I'm terrible. He wants me to leave but moms at church. Hopefully he'll change his mind before they get home. I love him so much. Why do I do that? Well, I don't have to leave just sleep on the coach. I need to learn to zip it. I love Chuck so much, what will I do if I lose Chuck? I know I'm not with Chuck for his money. Where was he when I first met him? I love Chuck for Chuck! I just wish I wouldn't speak sometimes. Aww, I really think I did it this time and to beat it all he told me to find somewhere to go and I smiled. Can you believe that! I would be devastated! I can't show my emotions. It aggravates me when I feel like crying and I smile. Well, he stayed mad at me for 24 hours, now he's over it, I just got to sleep on the coach. I bet I won't say he don't care again. After sleeping on the coach, I wake up to him giving me his ring back. He doesn't want to be married anymore. Me and my big mouth. You can't really blame him. I mean I never have his back. I do say some mean and hurtful stuff. He said he don't think he can take a lifetime of this. Agg, I hate it when I do stuff like that. I love him. He is the last thing I want to lose. I would be part of the 85%. It's a proven fact that 85% of all marriages of TBI patients end in divorce. Only 15% survive and most of them are the elderly. Well today is a new day. I'm going to stop being so mean and bite my tongue. I can change. That's what I'm telling myself over and over in my head. I can't even blame it on TBI. That's the sad part. Well, I sent this text to chuck. "I know I have a funny way of showing it, but I do love you. I'll call grandma to come get me after I take a shower to work on myself. It's kind of weird but I am more worried about you then me. You're the one that's going to be alone." Well, I'm at my mom's. I gave my ring back. I didn't want him to think I would actually keep it. I feel terrible. I ruined my marriage. Well, he made a comment one time that he was going to make me go over to my mom's as a lesson. I think Chuck don't think I remembered that, but I do, I hope that's all it is. If not change in plans is do. This book will be about divorce and there will be no house remodeling. I will walk without my walker, and I will finish this book and I will finish college. I will, I will, I will.

Now I know why the divorce rate is so high among TBI patients. Chuck is so mad at me right now it's pretty apparent that I get mad and go off for every little thing and I did something I've always done, that makes me think it wasn't a TBI thing. I put my kids above Chuck. Everyone knows you can't put anyone over your husband. Especially since I can't really fault him. I hope he knows how much I love him. But like I said before. I want Chuck, I don't need Chuck. Well, I do need him emotionally. I have to say I'm glad to be home. Even though I have rules now. Chuck said the funniest thing, he said doing my housework is my job as a housewife, like getting Joshua off to school is my job as a mother. We are watching the first preseason game of the Jaguars. We're winning too. It would be nice if I could afford 5 or 6 box seats that are handicapped too. I would switch people around. He can have his night out with the guys. Donald and Stepenie, Red and Ashley, Mike and his girlfriend, Miranda and Mike, Cliff and Michelle, and Brian and Dana. 6 would be nice that way Joshua could bring a friend. Boy I'll be glad to see my grand babies tomorrow. Ashley comes over with the grandkids a lot. Since I've been with my mom, I've haven't seen them but at church and you don't get to spend much time with them in church. I miss them little buggers. I had a good first day back. Chuck and I went to Ihop for breakfast. That's my favorite breakfast place. I had white chocolate chip and raspberry with raspberry sauce pancake grand slam breakfast. Man, it was good. Then we came home, cleaned house and went to Mike and Miranda's. Notice how I came home and did my job. Oh well, it is what it is. A guy at the Ihop had a shirt that said " Second Commandment. ", I don't know about the Commandment part, but I got this TBI thing. I am the only person I know that almost died in a car accident. They sent me to hospice and was planning my funeral one day. I came back to be an Author of a book. I am untouchable. If I do that physical therapy thing, I'm definitely untouchable. Red Lobster is my favorite dinner place. I usually always get maple chicken. Isn't that hilarious. A seafood place and I always get maple chicken. That is like the best chicken you can get, and you can only get it at Red Lobster. And Sonic is where I like to eat lunch. I get my milkshakes there. Steak-n-shake is probably just as good, but I pass by a Sonic all the time. It would be nice to have gift certificates to my favorite places.

After I got my phone, I forgot what I was going to say. Oh yeah, I remember what I was going to say. Chuck Wendyified the house. He put bars up everywhere, He handicapped proofed my whole house. There's one bar in my bathroom. That I want to put in 2 more. I would tell you all about it, but I would be breaking a rule. I will tell you this I'm keeping all my safety bars up. We're not getting any younger. Well, the kitchen, I'm not keeping the bars up in there. But I can touch where there's countertops less than arm length. But I will have a shower bench built in my bathtub. Will we love it or list it? I would love my house to be featured in one of them HGTV shows. /Chuck is mad once again. He said I keep going on and on about what I want to do to this house, and we don't even have it paid off yet. Well, he does have a valid point. It's what's mine is yours and yours is mine not what's mine is mine and what's yours is mine. Well Chuck just told me that with $200,000.00 we would be able to pay the house off, do all the remodeling, and still have enough to spend 50 thousand dollars. Wonder what a decent Author makes for a decent book. Time to use Google. I got a new plan. I can't tell you though, I'd be breaking a rule.

Chapter 16: Going to North Carlina

I'm so excited! I'm going to North Carolina for my Aunt Vickie and Uncle Dons 50th wedding anniversary, there renewing their vows. Happy Anniversary! We are going to spend the night at my cousin Penny's in Georgia also. It's going to be fun. I can't wait! See, Aunt Vicki and my mom are best friends. They're not really my aunt and uncle. We just call them that, and their kids are my cousins. They always swapped kids during the summer. I have a lot of memories of them. I got to spend the night at my cousin Sherry's house. My cousin Sherry gave me a Mickie Mouse coffee cup with a lid. The best part about it is it's Mickey Mouse. That's Jimmies favorite. Now every morning I drink my coffee in my Mickie Mouse coffee cup that Jimmie can't have. I'll look at him and do my ah ha a haha and he'll just look at me and whine. I know I'm mean. Trust me, he has everything he needs at Nana's and Papa's. / I'm going to make a sign that says no whining and crying at Nana's and Papa's house. I think it would be more accurate if I just put no crying around papa. To be honest they really don't care if Chuck isn't there. And one that says, "no sagging at nana's and papa's house". I don't care who doesn't want to hear it. I would have hooks on it and belts hanging on it. I could go to the Good Will and get them. / Well Miranda, I'm finally excited about coat hangers. I thought she was crazy one day. You should have seen her so excited over coat hangers. Well now I am that excited. They have this material that everything sticks to, so your clothes won't fall off and they are very thin and don't take up much room.

Well, it was Labor Day weekend, and we went to Dana and Brian's Saturday. Church on Sunday and Joel's Monday. It has definitely been a boring summer. We haven't gone on the boat once. That's why we need a boat of our own. We haven't gone in the pool much because Chuck works so much, the pool is green most of the time. That's why pool maintenance would be very helpful. It really sucks that we didn't have anything really exciting to do for Labor Day. We usually do something really cool for the weekend of Labor Day. I guess no one wants to hang out with a handicap. / Jimmies at that super cute stage where he's interested in everything. And man, he's your best friend if you got food. I love him to death. He's so cute. Facebook has this saying by handicap this. " The past is where you learn your lesson the future is where you apply the lesson". They also said "The smallest step in the right direction ends up being the biggest of your life. Tip toe if you must but take the step." The new me is going to be a better me. I promise. I'm going to write this book. Make enough to pay this house off and remodel it. Go back to school for physical therapy and do physical therapy. I already got my therapy room set up. Chachinng. I'm all set. The TBI page has this "If you stumble, make it part of the dance." I like that one. Here is another one from handicap this. "Sometimes what your students need most, right now, has nothing to with what's in the lesson plan. Sometimes they need encouragement". That's one thing I can offer that nobody else can because I've been through it and overcome it. Here's another one but I don't know who posted it." Never allow anyone or anything to drag you back to where God has delivered you from." I thought that was pretty good. / Someone said something about my house remodel. She said is my book still about my house remodel. Just for that I'm going to put more in here and I'm going to put it right here not where you can skip over it. Tell me! The living room will be in a light turquoise color almost a baby blue color and the kitchen will be in that color too, but I will add a brownish orange color just in the kitchen. My house is going to be beautiful.

Well today is 9/11. It's a day I'll never forget. It was a very sad day. I was sitting at the kitchen table at Mary's and Charlies when I saw the news. I had to go to their back porch and cry. That was a very sad day. / Dr. Shaw taught me to have a SMART plan. S-specific, M- measurable, A- achievable, R- realistic, and T- timely. He got a doctor's degree after two TBI's. That's encouraging. That just means I can go back to college. / Ashley must have read my book. She gave me the encouragement that I needed. She told me most Authors take 1 to 2 years to write a book. My S M A R T plan I'll be done in one yr. So, that's encouraging. She also stayed away one evening, I got a lot done on my book. She knows me so well. / Sometimes I want to cry, and I can't cry. It's sad. Since my accident I can't cry. I have no tears. Do you know how it feels to be sad and can't cry? Chuck thinks I should start taking Zoloft again. I say if your life is going through a rough patch you learn to deal with it. The depression comes and goes. Most of the time I am happy. I think when I'm around people, that makes me happy. Don't get me wrong some people really need medication. / I just heard some bad news. Brenda had a seizure while she was driving. They took her driver's license away. That's terrible! Brenda, if I get my way, which I will. I'll get my driver to take you where-ever you need to go. Which I get my way, you just got to have a little faith.

There I go rubbing my knee again like it's hurting or something. It used to hurt but it doesn't now. Wonder if it's a sign of healing. / A year after my accident, I had an I'm alive party, on the weekend closest to July 25th. I had an I'm alive cake and everything. When mom was getting the cake, the woman asks her why I'm alive and not I'm a survivor. Mom said that's just what she wants. A lot of the people I care about were there. I couldn't do it last year the money wasn't there but I'm thinking about making it an annual event. / I just got to say God has really been working on my heart about tithing and something else too. I am really in love with my Bible apps. Being a handicap, I can't carry much so having the Bible on my phone really helps. If someone sees me on my phone at church, it doesn't always mean I'm not paying attention. They also send me a notification with a Bible verse a day. / Unbelievable that someone with a diffuse axonal brain damage can be an Author of her own book and maybe own her own business from her home, physical therapist. That means I have brain damage all the way around on all lobes. Chuck just told me that. I just thought I have brain damage in the occipital lobe. The very back part of your brain. IDK, I think I'm pretty smart. This chick turned a negative situation and turned it into a positive. /I know that God made the hormone DHT to flood your body right before death. It makes you feel no pain or suffering. It calms you down, you're in a state of euphoria. Well, I don't know if it's like euphoria. Just because you want something to be true doesn't mean it is. / Chip and JoAnn Gaines have a new bed and breakfast, Chuck, I want to go to Texas! I want to sleep in their bed. / Right now, I am praying for my children, Ray I want the Lord to bring him a good woman, Ashley, that he will help her quit smoking and Joshua just that he grows up to be happy. Happiness, you can't ask for more than that. Well now I'm going to ask for happiness for all my kids.

Chapter 17: If you want to make God laugh make a plan

Chuck always says you want to make God laugh make a plan. Well, he certainly did put a stop to me becoming a nurse. I about died in a car accident! I don't think he laughs. I think I went through a terrible ordeal, but I think he uses that to do something very good. If I would not have gotten in the car accident, I wouldn't have been able to write this book and be a testimony for him. I am honestly happier now that I have gotten right with God. / In therapy, I have to do a test for the insurance company on how much I improved since I started. They consider me an old injury case. / Jimmies at that real cute stage where he'll drop stuff from his highchair and say, utto. Good thing we got an automatic vacuum cleaner, a dog. / TBI has one that says, 'I walk slowly, but I never walk backward". That one fits me to a T. Words of wisdom *post* " Don't ever let anyone break your soul. You have to stand on your own two feet and fight. There are people who would do anything to see you fail. Never give them the satisfaction. Hold your head up high. Put a smile on your face and stand your ground." I like that one. / Well Ashley and Red just gave me a long lecture on how I should be nicer to Chuck. IDK, I guess in my head I was right. You can only be nice for so long then you have got to stand up for what you believe in. Awe, now I feel terrible. I was just standing up for myself. I really didn't care what anyone says he was being a BAH before I sent a mean text to him. But it is what it is. It's done now, I can't go back and change it.

I know it sounds conceded and all, but I think Lisa might have quit her job for me. She always said I was her favorite patient. She went to my wedding and everything. For some reason, she could hardly look at me during my last visit. She is most definitely the best physical therapist ever! I don't think I would've passed that test for Medicare. They can't find the paperwork from the first test I did. I have to do so much better. I feel bad but the one thing I did learn is to make the best of every situation. I would hate it if Lisa did that for nothing. Lisa Leech is her full name. I promise I will do my best. Since Lisa isn't there, I'm going to go to the one by my house. The traffic is so bad going to the Southside, especially during rush hour traffic time. / They have this saying on Facebook. It's from TBI Hope and inspiration, a lot of the sayings are from them. "Success is not final, Failure is not Fatal, it is the courage to continue that counts. I thought that was pretty inspirational. They have another one by the same group. "Never give up on a dream because of the time it will take to accomplish it. The time will pass anyway." I think that is so true. / Why did this happen to me. I don't understand. I guess I'm having one of them feel sorry for yourself moments. Everyone treats me so different now. Like I'm special or something. Well, I guess I am. IDK just why? I guess I can be a testimony and write this book. / I tell everyone, don't let me go around with crooked pants. There was one boy, and his shorts were crooked and that's what I think about every time I see him. My mom goes around tugging me trying to straighten me up. She asked if I wanted her to stop doing it, and I told her if we are in public stop but if we're alone then do it. I don't want to be remembered as the girl with crooked pants. I don't want to be remembered as the smelly girl either. I always make sure I take a bath every day and put on a lot of deodorant. I use perfume too. Not too much though. Some people can't breathe if you put too much on. I don't want to make it to where people can't breathe. Breathing is important. / Well, I am sad to say Lisa died today. Lisa is Tommy's wife (Aunt Pat and Uncle Genes oldest son, Michelle's oldest brother). Tommy, I love you and Lisa will be forever missed. I know how much you loved her; she was the love of your life. I'm really sorry that cancer took her from you. One thing is for sure cancer doesn't discriminate. Well, today is Lisa's funeral and I'm at the house. That's why I need my own car with my own driver. Preferable someone not afraid of Chuck! Matter fact if you even show a sign of being scared, sorry but your fired. I liked Lisa. I can't believe I didn't go to her funeral. / I love ordering stuff in the mail. It's great! Because I forget a lot, I forget what I ordered. It's like I get a surprise in the mail. I love it. / I was told by Red an interesting thing. If you have to try to be nice then you're really mean. Idk, I never had to try to be nice before. I'm blaming that one on my TBI, most definitely. He's a man anyway what does he know. / There's this saying on Facebook from TBI that says, "little by little becomes a lot". I like that it's like slow and steady wins the race. Words of wisdom says "Just because a person smiles all the time doesn't mean their life is perfect. That smile is a symbol! Of Hope and Strength. " Here's one by TBI that says, "Face trouble with courage, disappointment with cheerfulness, triumph with humility". The same site says, "Strength is nothing more than how well you hide the pain". It also says, "Don't let someone dim your light, simply just because it shines in their eyes". Handicap this has one that says, "Don't stop until your proud". Don't worry I won't, I'm already proud and trust me I'm not stopping. After my accident, I had to make a new email and I picked wonderfulwendy. TBI also has one that says Strength shows, not only in the ability to persist, but the ability to start all over. Words of wisdom has a post that say's "My life isn't perfect, but I am thankful for everything I have". Isn't that the truth/ I think I'm harder on Joshua than anyone else. He's the one I have to get on to. It's my job, as a mother. It's a shame too. He's such a good boy and he does such a good job taking care of me. No child should have to go through what he has had to m a SPIAgo through with me and my accident. Poor kid, I feel sorry for him. His mom almost died, then he had to watch me go through the recovery. I know my accident affected everyone I was close too, but it affected Joshua more than the rest.

Chapter 18: I am a SPIA

OMG (that's for goodness. I don't take the Lord's name in vain). I should apologize. I just came to the realization that maybe my daughter is right. I am a SPIA, and I think the whole world should be about me. I can't believe what I did. I am ashamed of myself. I told Aubriella that I am the queen B of this house. And I said the real word too. Who would tell a three-year-old that? I feel horrible. I know some people that would never let their kids ever see their grandparents if they said that. I feel ashamed.

Well today is Lisa's birthday. Even though she's not with us anymore I would like to wish her happy birthday. She is cancer free. / I will rejoice because he has made me glad. The wheel of fortune of the week is " Are you looking or listening for Jesus or just reading the bible". I think the most important thing Jesus wants is for you to have a personal relationship with him. Talk to him and pray to him. He likes for you to go to church and all, but I don't think that's as important as a good relationship with him. I am not a good example. I do all kinds of stuff wrong, and I don't go to church like I should. Chuck says I'm a heathen. Chuck Larramore say what you want but the only time I seen you pick up a bible before my accident is when you were thinking about breaking up with me. That means you do have a personal relationship with him. And he wants us to be together. Ha! I like that. / Chuck, you said you got saved when you were in your early teens. Well, I believe once you're saved you're always saved. The question is, what if you stop believing? That I'm not too sure about.

I can't carry much so having the bible on my phone really helps. If someone sees me on my phone at church, it doesn't always mean I'm not paying attention. They also send me a notification with a bible verse a day. / A song can send a message all of its own. / They have the King James version Bibles on Audio. The Bible is the Bible I don't care if it's on your phone or audio. You can listen to that in the car when you're driving down the road or wireless headphones that you can listen to too while you're doing something else. I saw this somewhere; this older guy was telling this young girl they have audio on this book, but I can actually read. It's not for people who can't read, it's for people who are busy and don't have time to disconnect from the world long enough to read a book. / Ashley gave me this great idea. She said that people do U-tube blogs and make a lot of money. I think that's a good idea. After I finish this book, I will do a blog an inspirational about a TBI patient, a handicap at her everyday life.

I'm going to call it. I'm alive with TBI. I think that's a good name and a good idea. Chuck doesn't even want to talk about it. He's got more important things to handle right now. He says that I didn't do this for him. No, I'm doing this for us! Don't he realize I'm just trying to help us out, so he doesn't have to work all the time. It might be a long shot, but it couldn't hurt. Get me a selfie stick and hook it to my walker. It might help me with my problem of talking in front of people. Now that I sound all stupid, I don't like talking around people that much. I guess I'm afraid people aren't going to spend time with me. Well, if they can't understand me that might be a problem. I think my voice is getting a lot stronger. I'm going to try to keep my blog as non-religious as possible. I have a strong feeling I'm going to do a religious one later. Well with that last news Ashley told me (about having a blog) I can feel my head getting bigger and bigger. I got to get that under control. I don't think God would like that. And I don't think anyone that has an ego problem is all that attractive. Also, jealousy doesn't look good on anyone.

Jeff Foxworthy has this new game show out. I love it. It has a whole bunch of biblical questions on it. I learn a lot. The day is not wasted when I watch that show. The day is not wasted if you learn something new. I say that a lot now. I would really like to meet him, Jeff Foxworthy. / Well, I got some terrible news. I hate not being able to talk on the phone where people can actually be able to understand me. Tommy was in the hospital, and he had his phone. The bug man Tommy, I have two cousins name Tommy. He doesn't do text. I don't want to call him. I sound like a stupid retard. You can't understand me. With Tommy he's been battling with his blood sugar for years, He just wasn't paying attention to it that's all. But it could have been deadly. Pay attention Tommy. / I'm mad at Chuck again. It may be a TBI thing. But I asked him to make me a milkshake and he refused and just brought me a bowl of ice cream. I know it seems miner but it's burning me up.

My niece, Amber wrote on Facebook "If words could leave a scar would people be more careful of what they say". Yes, Amber I believe they would. I know I would anyway. That's a lesson I need to learn, unfortunately. She also said this one " Turning down the volume in life allows you to listen to God." Amber is very wise. / I'm disappointed with myself. I didn't go to church. No excuse. I could have called mom, several people but nooooo. Time to use my bible app and bible study app I downloaded. / I'm so excited, Chuck is coming home. I guess his guys got done early. So, I got him for two weeks minus a couple of days. / Today is the day after Halloween. I made Ashley mad at me, so I spent Halloween at home by myself. Joshua went trick or treating with his brother, sister and all grandkids, their other brother Damian, and his mom Maggie. This is probably his last year trick or treating. Me and my big mouth. Well at least he had a good time. That's what's important! Aubriella said you can't say mean things. I think there's a lot to learn from a cute 4-year-old. Well at least he had a good time. / God made me look the way I do and made my personality the way it is. Fault him, dare you. If I were boring no one would want to read my book. Anyway, there's nothing wrong with exercising, keeping healthy and looking your best. And I value everything God has given me. I'm not all about money. I just like having nice things. There's nothing wrong with that. I'd be happy living in a cardboard box. Not satisfied but happy.

Chapter 19: Satin's Holiday

I would like to do a haunted house or a tribulation house, one year. We can have Jimmie standing the other side of the fence where you go out giving out candy dressed up like chucky. He would make a cute Chucky. Everyone says Halloween is Satan's holiday. IDK, I don't think so. You get to dress up scary or like your favorite characters. I love it! Jimmie is so cute. He got a little pumpkin. Not super little, you can still carve it. He's been caring it around for days and this lady come up to him. She asked him if he was going to carve it and gave her a look and said no, he's my friend. The lady asked what his friend's name was, and he looked at her like she was stupid and said pumpkin. He got a diaper and wipes from his mom, and he said his pumpkin was dirty. He flipped it over and started wiping his butt and then he put the diaper on it. ROFL! I thought that was so funny. The looks he gives is something else. / There is a movie that I really like "Suicide Squad". I guess I am a big geek. With Harley Quinn. I know she is super bad, but I would like to think of myself as the good Harley Quinn. I can be fighting for God. / Someone was asking what it was like having TBI. I didn't understand then, but I do now. It's like having a brain fog all the time. It's frustrating when I can't remember something that just happened. And what really is hateful I have all my other disabilities so everything I do is so difficult. / You know I've been reading back at all I've done. I can't even remember any of the things I supposedly said. I know I must of, I wrote about it. I wouldn't lie about it. It makes me look bad. / Idk, it's probably my imagination. I'm an emotional wreck. I feel like no one wants to hear me speak. Like I'm a loudmouth or something.

Chuck is such a BAH. He keeps going on and on about all he is going to do to the house. He doesn't have the money either. If I can't talk about it, he shouldn't talk about it either. This is God's plan. What do you got to say about that! To his defense he has worked really hard on his credit. He has really good credit. He is very good with money. He can get a home equity loan and what he wants to do will bring the property value up. / I was told once again maybe the new me needs a walker. I'm definitely not satisfied with that! But that's what the speech therapist said about my voice too. Well, I definitely don't sound the same. My voice is definitely stronger now, but I personally think that I sound stupid. At first, my voice was so light you could hardly hear me. If all I need is to build more core muscle, then that's not permanent. Walking next door to Dana's with a gate belt that's safe and it made my core muscles hurt. I don't care what they say, I will walk again with no walker. If muscle is what I need then Muscle is what I'll get. I used more muscles doing that than any of the exercises that the therapist gave me to do and going to the gym, so I say do it. I'm not saying I'm ready to go with no walker at all but walking to Dana's with my gate belt is good exercise. / I miss the old me. Today is my last day of therapy. It feels like everyone has given up on me. Chuck and I aren't the same either. I know he loves me, but he's taken care of me for so long. I guess he's taken the care giver role. We used to have so much fun together! I miss that. I'm just having another one of them feel sorry for yourself couple of days. I haven't taken any Zoloft. I figure if life throws you curve balls, you just learn how to deal with it. / They said that it's bad to skip breakfast, especially if you're dieting. I don't get it, that's more calories and your metabolism get started. I'm going to google that. Well, I did, it said because you get hungry faster, and you tend to snack on high calorie foods. / Chuck said something else about my book. He said nobody wants to hear about my life before the accident. Now he's just being a B.A.H. He said nobody wants to hear about my life before my accident and I have a lot of my life before the change. Well, I beg to differ, Sharon asked me if I was going to put my life before my accident and she gave me thumbs up. Ah ha ah ha as Jimmie and I would say. Let me write the book. It is an autobiography. I think I was pretty interesting before and I am interesting now. / Oh yeah, I got to tell you this. Chuck as admitted to reading this book, so he only said a couple of things about the house remodeling.

Today I went to the 3 month follow up appointment for my eye doctor's appointment. I saw Berry at the twin towers. The valley parking guy. He asked surprised I knew his name. He'll remember me when the time is right. The eye doctor said I need laser surgery on my left eye, and I'll be 20\20. I hope he's right. I'd hate to give twin towers a bad rep. other than the waiting game, I like the place. / Chuck is envious he asked the eye doctor how she has 20/20 vision and she need glasses when she first come home from the hospital. He told him they were for double vision. I lose my glasses so much. I can hardly read without my reading glasses. Well, it has gotten a little better, but I still have a hard time seeing writing and my computer. Chuck, you can't win. If I'm not going to have reading glasses on my head, I'm going to want good sunglasses. Cheap dollar store glasses just aren't going to do it. I want Ray bans, Maui Jim's or Oakley's. As a matter of fact if I need reading glasses (which I am getting old) I want a pair of sunglasses with reading glasses in it. That just proves doctors can't keep you from getting old. I had the very best doctors trying everything they could think of and I'm still getting old. Actually, I would like a pair of bifocals that are reading glasses and the rest of them are clear so when I want to play on my phone and watch tv I won't look stupid with my glasses on the end of my nose.

My head hurts when I start to type so I'm going to go for now. I stopped playing games on my phone because my head hurts so bad. Like Trivia Crack and Sudoku, well I still play Sudoku every now and then. I play a lot of solitaire. I play a lot of word games as well. At least I can see it. It gives me a headache still but at least I can see. / Just because I say what I feel doesn't mean I'm a bad person it just means I'm straight up. I'm sorry if I come across as mean. / I notice a lot of people avoid me. Probably because they can't understand me or just don't want to be around a handicap. / Michelle came over with baby Colby. Michelle said I looked like I've been losing weight. Cliff, you did a good job picking her. I knew I liked her. / I hurt my leg. I hurt it under my knee. It's a sharp pain and sometimes it goes all the way down to my ankle. It went behind me when I fell. I think it's my nerve. It's not swollen. I know I didn't break a bone. It doesn't hurt when I stand on it, just when I move it. I have to admit. I stopped using my walker around the house for a little while. I just couldn't do steps and curbs. Well, the head honcho, Chuck said use my walker from now on, so I will use my walker from now on. What choice do I have? It hurts so bad. Chuck said he was going to make a doctor's appointment. So, we'll see what the doctor says. / I think that you can be bikers and have tattoos all over and boys with long hair can be the nicest people. Well, my dad kind of burst my bubble on the tattoo thing. He said it says in the bible that you shouldn't put permanent markings on your body. I can't find it.

Chapter 20: I need a BAH to make me listen

Chuck only takes me being a SPIA for so long. Then he gets serious. You got to know your limitations. The good Lord knows I need a BAH to make me listen. / Well, Chuck got so mad at me last night he had to leave. He was being a BAH for real. / I have great news. You know that walker I was going to get from Brooks and Medicare wouldn't pay for all of it, well our cost is $250.00. The one that goes behind you. I'm getting it for Christmas. Chuck said he usually doesn't tell me, but I won't remember anyway. What he doesn't know is I have selective memory. I'll remember. / Chuck said something very disturbing. I was baking cookies and I thought I could get them out, but I jerked, and cookies went all over the oven. Anyway, he said there are somethings I will never be able to do. The word never just echoed in my head. I just never thought this condition was permanent. Like walking, I will be able to walk without my walker. But drink without a lid or carry a plate. Nooo, stupid dystonia. It makes me wonder how many phones and tablets I'm going to break in my lifetime. Idk if I'm going to be able to do the therapy thing or not. Well maybe I could just run an outsource of Brooks. Like having Lisa or Nikki or someone else work at a private spa like retreat physical therapy. I would have scented candles and everything. I would have the best security. I just want everyone to have the same awesome experience that I had. I would have a day for water aerobics and art day. Even a game day. \ I'm glad I went from being a nurse to physical therapy. I would hate to have a nurse like me giving me a shot. With a little jerk. I actually was into physical therapy before I went into nursing. Nurses made more money. I guess I was all about money. I think I would enjoy physical therapy more. Oh well. I might not have the opportunity to do either now. But I always was interested in physical therapy. I remember all of the physical therapist that come to Mary's house. I always said that would be a good job. I would get paid for keeping fit. Now I would rather travel than go back to school. I had a hard-enough time before my Traumatic Brain Injury. Maybe I can visit the missionaries in other countries. That would be fun. / I'm not doing so good with controlling my walker. I still kick it and it always goes off in one direction and I don't stay in the walker like I'm supposed too, Operator error, I guess. Nikki used to say that about me kicking my walker. I used to say stupid walker and she would tell me it's an operator error.

I went to the twin towers today for laser eye surgery. It was quite painless and quick. I still need my reading glasses. That's like my new thing anyway. I got a pair to go with every outfit. It didn't hurt, and

I can see just as good as when I went in there. I found one of them neat saying on the wall all around Shans at the twin towers. It's "Kindness is something a deaf man can hear, and a blind man can see". I like that! We went to country Cabin the restaurant after that. It's good to treat yourself every now and then. I'm not all about what's in style. For instance, I would never want to move into a tiny house. I would be happy but not satisfied. I like having a lot of stuff. I want everything I need at my fingertips. That's not to mention the stuff I want that I don't really need. They do have some tiny houses that are pretty cool. I wouldn't mind designing my son, Ray a tiny house. That would be cool. He can have one on wheels, that way he could take it anywhere. Well, I messed my arm up walking on the treadmill. I usually put the harness on, but Joshua and Chuck were at football practice every night! I was by myself all day until 8 or 9 o'clock at night. Anyway, I was determined to get better. I was walking without the harness on every night for an hour. Well, I fell and hurt my arm. I could tell It wasn't broke. About two weeks after I fell, I went to the doctors. After I got X-rays of my arm, the doctor told me I had degenerative arthritis. I'm not that old! But the doctor told me to exercise, and it would make it better so that's what I'm doing. We'll I just started exercising it again. After I exercised it, it hurt worse, so I stopped exercising it. After that it stopped hurting at all for a day or two. I didn't exercise during the whole time, and it started to hurt again. So, this time I am exercising it continually, see if it'll stop hurting and stay not hurting.

Chapter 21: Nighttime activities

Now that Chuck is gone, I'll tell you about my schedule for my nighttime activities. On Monday night, I do my thigh master thing, watching TV. I do two reps of three different kinds. I do 50 a rep. First, I do the thighs, then I do the stomach, that really works. I stopped doing 400 sit ups when I started doing that. I went from 400 to 200 my stomach started hurting. I was afraid it would turn hard. One big ball of muscle, Ewe. I have concluded that I have to do sit ups and I have to go on a diet to have a flat stomach. Then, I do my arms. On Tues, I do my exercise bicycle for an hour, On Wed I do my treadmill. That's why I had to wait to tell you. Chuck would be mad if he knew I was doing my treadmill without my harness. On Thurs., I do my thigh master thing. On Fri., I ride my bicycle. I got Ray Ray, Red, Dad, and Chuck to take me for a walk as extra. I am on the go from the time I get up till the time I go to bed. I am sick and tired of people acting like I don't do anything! I go all day long. I don't know why, but I hate, hate people telling me I can't do something. It's like with college and redoing my house, it just makes me want to do it more. I will do all these things. I don't care! People make me so mad with their negative ways and opinions! Just leave me alone and let me do it. It does take forever for me to do anything. Like cleaning and stuff takes me forever. But I get faster every time. The simplest things like brushing my teeth and making my bed take forever. I don't want anyone to think I exercise all day long. That last little bit made it seem like that, that's just not what I want to be known for. Don't get me wrong, I exercise a lot, but happiness is what's important. Happiness is what matters. I will never ever choose exercise over shopping or spending time with the grandkids. As a matter of fact I want to start a new exercise with Jimmy on a motorcycle with a long handle. I'll walk to and around the cul-de-sac and back home. It's good to exercise but exercising your faith is very important. / Chuck bought me a bell. It's gold and says ring for a drink. I love it! / Nortavac has this workout machine. It has an Ipad on it, with a personal trainer. I want one of those. I would make room in my workout room for that machine. They have one with a bicycle. I would like to start doing yoga too. I'm a little afraid that I can't do everything but most of yoga I should be able to do. I would like to try Pyo also. I want one of them ZAAZ wellness evolved. This one lady said I was twerking when I was on it.

My phone is supposed to be shatter resistant and waterproof. Well, I broke it. I guess, I proved it's not wendyproof. / I just want to say I miss my flip flops. That's ALL I use to wear all year round. I had a pair to match every outfit. I would get irate if you wore my flip flops. Ask my daughter. Good flip flops leave your footprint. There, like figure prints everyone is different. I really miss not being able to talk where you can understand me. I have noticed that people just act like I'm not saying anything. I miss not driving too. Well to be honest I don't miss driving. I just miss not being able to go when I want to go. I also get tired of making a mess. I hate the way I make a mess all the time. I snort now too. It's so embarrassing when I snort in church. I get lost in my phone also. I play a lot of games. At least they're cognitive games. I don't like carbonated sodas either. There not good for you anyway, I just thought it was odd. I'm going to the park with Michelle and Z, that's Joseph's little boy. Joseph is Michelle's sister Debbie's son. Aubriella will like that. / Oh, by the way, Joshua has halitosis. That means bad breath. We have a lot of fun together. / Wilburn and Wilburn are singing at Church today. They are an excellent singing group. They sing that song about kicking God out of your school, I didn't cause your pain. I don't know the name of it, but it goes something like this " isn't the one to blame. He didn't cause your pain. You ask him to leave." They were even on the news. You can look them up online and buy one of their CD's. That's what I'm going to do. They also sing a song that was on Facebook by Pentonix. Mary, did you know. I love that song. Pentonix had that song on Facebook. / I really love the way Miranda Lambert is not afraid to show her faith, Duck Dynasty is also a show that is not afraid to show their love for the Lord. / Well Valerie is gone. It was nice having her company for a little while anyway. / Good news I am going to the mountains for thanksgiving. Well, it's very unfortunate, Chuck has to work through Thanksgiving. We were going to take a drive and go see all the Larramore's in Lakeland. But since he's got to work, I get to spend Thanksgiving with my family. They are renting a cabin in the mountains for five days. I'm so excited! It's Monday now come Wednesday I will be mountain bound. Me and Joshua can't wait. I just found out that I am going on a cruise. I'm double excited. In the perfect little world in my somewhat psychotic mind this book will be published before I go on my cruise and I will come back to a remodeled house done by Chip and JoeAnn Gaines, well maybe the property brothers. Who am I kidding, our cruise is supposed to last 9 days! You can't do a remodel in 9 days? Anyway, my house my way, I'll remodel it. I know this is going to sound crazy. But I signed up to get a disability dog. I will have to spend two weeks in Orlando, so you can get used to the dog. Now I want a miniature pig. When I was a kid, I wanted a miniature pig. My dad brought me home a Ginny pig. That's not a pig! Well, we can all go to Disney World to get my new miniature pig. I just found out that Tommy's daughter Nikki is selling miniature pigs, that's interesting, that's something I'm going to have to think about. / I would like to buy my kids and grandkids annual passes to Disney World as stocking stuffers. That would be so awesome.

Chapter 22: North Carolina

Well, we're leaving tomorrow to go to Chimney Rock in North Carolina. I'm so excited! I under packed for my trip to go see Chuck. So, I over packed for this trip. My dad is going to be mad. Oh well better off to be overly packed than not pack enough. I can't wait. My dad didn't get mad, but my mom had something to say about it. I found out the elevator is broken at Chimney Rock and they would rather shop than climb a big mountain. So, retail therapy it is. It wore me out, but it was fun. I am very thankful I have a wonderful family. Well, it's the day after Thanksgiving. Everyone went to some Tavern. My mom didn't feel like going so she stayed home with me. I'm glad everyone didn't stay home because of me. I would've felt terrible. Instead, I took a long Jacuzzi bath, ate left over thanksgiving dinner and took a long nap, after that mom and dad took me to look at the Christmas lights at the Chimney Rock shopping strip. Then I came home watch Florida \Seminole game. Isn't sibling rivalry great. I am a Seminole fan only because I grew up in a house full of male gator fans and I liked the colors garnet and gold better than orange and blue. I've got to be different. Now my husband is a Gator fan. Well David didn't say much, like he enjoyed me being there, but he was mad the Gators lost and I'm sure he could've lived without having me run my mouth. The Siminoles won yea! What a great day. One of my brothers told me something that piqued my interest. They were talking about a charger that was magnetic. You don't have to fight plugging it in all the time. That's something worth having. I mess up so many phones and chargers because I can't plug them in. / I am home, and I just got to say I miss my grandkids. Jimmie is so funny. He stills my walker, and he was trying to get my cup out of the basket, so I tell Aubriella to get my cup he throws himself down and the fit begins. I offer to share but he wants the whole cup, so I just bust out laughing (BOL). Lol, A few minutes later he comes up and gives me a big hug. That's my buddy for you. / I bought this new Christmas painting it has this saying on it" Dear Santa... I want it all!" I thought that was appropriate. It's beginning to feel a lot like Christmas. I downloaded this new screensaver. It's got this light up Christmas tree and it says how many days till Christmas. We got 15 days left. I just got to say. I'm proud of my son, Ray. He is doing so good with money. He got his own place and everything. I went to go see RayRay's new place over the weekend. He has a real nice little place. I'm so proud of him.

I hate to say it but I'm going to have to switch teams. I went to UF doctors and everything. The new me is going to have to go with a new team. I am a Gator fan now. Like I said before I feel like humpty dumpty. UF, which is the gators, did an excellent job of putting me all back together again. I can't go against them. This is not a good start as a Gator fan, they're losing. The Gators got stomped. Chuck is telling me if this is what's going to happen, I can just stay an FSU fan. And this year FSU beat the Gators. I would have had bragging rights for a whole year. / I got this candle holder that says " I can do all things through Christ who strengthens me. " The candle I got to go in it is pumpkin for the holidays. Actually, Ashley bought it I don't why I said that. That reminds me of when I told a lie to my mom, I don't even remember what it was about I just remember that I wasn't trying to hide anything. There was no reason to lie. Mom gave me a good chewing out over that. I tell you I'm not a very good example. I just thought about something, none of this is about me. Not the accident, nothing. Well, that gives me something to think about. Things should get really interesting. Also, I just want to tell Uncle Marshal that I know and I'm doing everything possible. He gave me a look when I was leaving last time. I didn't know it then, but I know what the look was about now. It was like he wanted to tell me something but didn't want to get involved. Well, I know. Your nephew is kind of stubborn, but I'll do my best. / I had an awesome time at Miranda's for the new year. I never feel different with her. Well, I'll be happy to tell you and Chuck that I downloaded a stopwatch app from that neat app the play store". Now I can time my rest periods to 3 minutes. Lisa said to wait 2 and a half to 3 minutes in between on my reps but when Liz asked, she said there wasn't a time limit. She just gave me that cause if she didn't, I wouldn't rest. You hear that Chuck! / I'm not doing so good with controlling my walker. I still kick it and it always goes off in one direction and I don't stay in the walker like I'm supposed too. Operator error.

Chapter 23: Christmas

Well, I went to Chucks company Christmas party at Dave and Busters. It was a lot of fun but once again it made me realize how different I really am. Well today is Christmas! I got my new walker, actually it was delayed in the Christmas rush mail order. It's okay I am a big girl. I got a selfie stick, a button for the selfie stick, a cute little stuffed bear from Chuck. Its soft, move over frog. I also got a microwavable bacon tray and oven gloves. Now all I need a pan that has a lid that goes in the oven. Wouldn't you know the BAH, Chuck, don't like microwave bacon. Well, cook it yourself then. / Chuck says I'm ungrateful. I got my new walker yesterday. I know it helps me learn how to walk without my walker and it helps with my posture. The other walker I will let it get pushed out in front of me and I'll be all bent over. I seem to kick the other one too. But... It is a lot harder. As if things aren't hard enough as it is but I know it is best for me and it will get easier in time, so I just need to toughen up and just do it. Like Nike says. I would like to buy me a whole bunch of Nike, just do it outfits. / Well, I'm so disappointed in myself. I lied again today, and I don't even know why. Pretty bad when your daughter is telling you how wrong it is. I am not a good example. God and everyone like someone that's truthful. No one likes someone that you can't believe anything they say because they're always lying. / Good thing I got my stuff to start my blog. I was just looking on Google on how much Authors make and not a whole lot. I'm going to need more than what Google says if I'm going to pay this house off and remodel this house. We are going to Lakeland tomorrow for two days. Well, that gave me a lot to think about with the Google thing on how much this book is going to make. My plan isn't to S M A R T now. I had a doctor's appointment with Dr. Alvarez, my primary physician. He's a good doctor. He's very thrall. For some reason, my lower neck is starting to hurt and my knee that I'm always rubbing is hurting too. A double whammy. Preexisting injury, the doctor said. / I'm sorry to say that I broke that coffee cup that Sherry gave me. The Mickey mouse one. Don't worry Sherry, I'll still think of you.

I got it all figured out in my somewhat psychotic mind. Step-by-step, how I'm going to get Laura down here and all. What, the grand babies need her too. A child can never have too much love. / I got to say that they are crazy! I just googled how much I should weigh for my age and height. They said I was obese, and I should only weigh 97lbs. I would look sick if I lost that much weight. I say just look in the mirror and work on whatever you have a problem with. I would like to work on my stomach. My stomach is really the only place I have a problem with. I weigh 151and I think if I can get to 130ish I'd look great. So, my diet, well I guess I'm not really on one. I just watch what I eat and don't overly eat. / I figured something out. You have got to have the correct timing. If it's the wrong timing, it's not going to work. It will all blow up in your face. There was a man that come up to me and I had a crowd around wanting to shake my hand. Well, he told me that he was an atheist and now he is a born-again Christian. He said it like I needed to talk to him. Well, I do want to talk to you. That was God getting you to come up to me. Isn't it exciting, your part of a much bigger picture? I'm going to try to have a book signing event at my church one Saturday. Please come. I'll buy you lunch or dinner. I'm going to have volunteers come and sing. We have an excellent group of singers. A good song can have a message of its own. I think I'm going to get Bro. Terry Mattison to help me with that. He is the choir director at church. He's also the preacher's assistant. He was the youth director before that and when I was a teen. I'm going to give 10% right off the top to the church and split the rest of it between me and some origination that has helped me through my accident. I said something in this book that was the wrong timing and I feel really bad for it. / Everyone at my church says I got a Cadillac of a walker. It's a bright turquoise blue color and everything. My new walker has a seat on it too. It's fancy.

Chapter 24: Everything cost money

I just realized that everything I want just costs money. God says money is the root of all evil, 1st Timothy 6:10. I just don't get it. It might be, but I don't want enough to have a nice house and have what I need and want. IDK, money is what makes the world go around. It takes money to make money. I think it's all according to what you do with it. I can't imagine someone being evil and they give a lot to the missionaries or something. The pastor said something about money, but I don't exactly remember the exact words, but he basically says that if you don't let it control your happiness money don't hurt. / Sometimes I feel really stupid. Like now, I can't even find out how much money is on my child support card. I keep putting the card number in wrong. I'm such a retard. Just kidding, I'm really smart I just don't move like I'm supposed to. / Man, Agg. Chuck said it's going to cost me like a hundred thousand dollars to get a publisher. Well, that kind of burst my bubble. Well, I want to put so much back out of my child support every week. I'm never going to give up. I can promise you that. Quitters never win or prosper. I don't think he knows anyway. What does he know? If he's right, then I need to change professions. It's been a few weeks, but I felt compelled to write in here. Oh, I got to tell you what I got for Valentine's Day. I got a new phone, the Galaxy 6 and a new charger. One of the ones you can just put your phone on. Wish they had a notebook charger like that. Anyway, my case is supposed to be guaranteed, to be Wendy proof. They don't know me too well, obviously. / I want to go see the movie" Heaven's gift". I kind of feel I am a gift of God.

I got a change in my design plan. I'm breaking a rule but, oh well. I've never been good at following rules, especially from a boy anyway. On the add on addition instead of having a dining room, I'm going to keep that as the kid's playroom. We are not very formal people and we do have the eat in nook. I can always get a portable fold out table to put up when I have the family over. In the playroom I want to put a train track at the top where the boarder is, sort of like the boarder. Then, I want to paint halfway down with chalk board paint and have a little ledge at the top, so I can keep the chalk, it can be like the chair rail. That way the grandkids can always color. Then I want to put a racing car track that you can lower over their little table. Then I'll keep the therapy room. Do it up in Jaguars. I want something on the ramp down. They got this show on TV where they make anything you want into an aquarium. I would put aquarium as a ramp going down to the lower portion of the house. That's going to be so cool. I would bring my Jaguar and therapy session in it, put that in as decoration. I would also have a dry island portion. That way Jimmie will have a spot for lizards and frogs and stuff. He's always catching frogs. I almost bought him a bearded dragon lizard for his birthday. He would love that. Well maybe I should get a frog and lizard that's good with water. I would like to build a bathroom in the bedroom in the add on edition, that way it will go outside to the pool.

I have a secret, I know things. I don't know everything just what God wants me to know. I didn't tell anyone when I knew things before, now I'm telling the whole world with this book. Now that I think about it, I don't think I had premonitions before. I think it was God. I'm going to be known for my house remodel. I can't believe it. I'm going to get my house remodeled. I'm so excited. / I have decided I don't want to go back to school to be a physical therapist. It's a women's prerogative to change her mind. I'll still have water aerobics day and art day. I'm also going to start a Missionaries need nice houses too foundation. I will go all over the world and give missionaries nicely decorated and remodeled homes. Out of all the people I know Chuck is the one person that could start a foundation like that. He might not now but he can figure it out. Between him and Miranda, if they put their heads together, they can do it. I can be a gadabout. I've been dying to use that word since Mrs. Howard told me that word a few years before my accident. She named her boat that. Gadabout means – a person who travels often to many different places. I thought if you have a traumatic Brain injury you were stupid, I think I'm pretty smart. Okay back to the story Wendy. I am also going to flip houses for a living. I know just who is going to sponsor it. Like I said before, it takes money to make money. Now, I need to find me a Jessie. I would like to flip houses in downtown Jacksonville and maybe San Marco. I don't know that but downtown has some beautiful old houses that just need some love. I know other things too. I'm only telling my family. They're the only ones that matter anyway. It's hateful having your own family not believe you. I just got some terrible news. I just found out that Miss Higgins died. The Higgins are missionaries to Mexico, and they are from our church. Now it's getting personal. I know, I'm going to dedicate my Missionaries Need Nice Houses Too foundation to her. Let me tell you children of Missionaries go through a lot too. They are uprooted from their families, grandparents and Aunts and Uncles. / What's going to happen with this book? I guess I am a big dreamer. This book isn't going to pay my house off and do the remodeling. I don't even think I'll make enough to pay it off. They have this saying on Facebook "If you can dream it, you can do it". Well between this book and my blog I'm going to start doing it. I'm not going to quit I can tell you that. I'm not a quitter. Quitters never wins or prospers.

Chapter 25: I watch a lot of movies

My mom says if she doesn't do anything else, she always makes her bed. That way if anyone asks her what she did that day, she can always tell them she made her bed. / I watch a lot of movies. Before I go on, I just got to say I will never run out of movies to watch. I remember when I was growing up, I had 7 channels. Then I got cable. Now I have so many movies it's unreal. Even though if you ask a teenager, they never have anything to watch. I just want to say I love Pure Flix. They have really good clean movies. That's so hard to find now days. They also have Christian based movies. / I watch a movie every night at suppertime. I really like "Annie". The one with Jamie Fox in it. It's not very often that they make an old-time favorite over and it's just as good or better. I really don't know, I watched Annie when I was in my teens, and it was pretty old fashion then. The other one I like is "inside out". It's a good one to watch with the grandkids. Miss Reilly Rain reminds me of sadness, and madness, she gets so mad sometimes. There's not madness in the movie his name is anger. Jimmie reminds me of meanness. There's no meanness either, it just fits him. / I'm in an uproar over this racial crap going on. I just don't get it. Regardless of whether they are white, African American, Mexican, Russian, or whatever, you don't judge a person by what they look like, you judge them by their character and personality. And let me tell you racism goes both ways. I've been called a white cracker on more than one occasion and I'm nice to everyone. So, I do know how it feels. Let me tell you something that just happened to my son that really burns me up. He (Joshua) had to do an oral report on slavery at school where he had to stand up in front of the class and he used the word black instead of the word African American. Well, there were two "African American" boys he had been friends with since grade school in his class. They got mad at him and said that he was racist. They haven't been friends since. Well, I just got to tell you son you're not missing out, He wasn't really your friend anyway.

That reminds me of something someone told me. They said that you get them with a group of your own kind and if you have a problem with one of them that they will all turn against you every time. It doesn't matter how tight you think you might be with them. My kind is African American. Well, my goal is to prove them wrong! I'm always nice to everyone and they are always nice to me back. And I will continue to be.

Who knows I may never really know? / Ok, back to the incident with my son. I did not know that! If that didn't happen, I would have made a whole bunch of people mad at me. I just went back and changed the words. Not trying to make anyone mad here. I just didn't know and neither did Joshua. You know what, I heard if you say something three times to someone it's suggestive hearing. Well, I'm going to do an experiment. I'm going to say best seller three times and see if it works. Chuck's cousin Paul said it once at Aunt Ann's funeral. Thanks Paul! I've been obsessed with it ever since. That doctor suggested writing a book one time. I didn't even think about it before that. Maybe you only have to hear it once.

I just watched Maddia's Christmas and it said something about saying the black word in the movie. That's not the first time I watched that movie either. I didn't notice it the first time. It doesn't matter what color you are. That reminds me of a Sunday school song." Red, or yellow, black or white, they are precious in his sight. Jesus loves all the little children of the world." That's how the song goes people. If you're going to get mad over the black word, get mad at the person who wrote it. I think we all need to practice that one rule "Love thy neighbor." Media is so funny. Everyone needs a good R.O.T.F. (roll on the floor laugh) every now and then. I laugh with my stupid sounding voice and everyone else just laughs harder. Don't worry I'm glad I can give other people a good laugh. Everyone loves a good laugh. I also love Keven Hart. Joshua is so funny. He thinks he's the white Keven Hart. I would really like to meet him. He's so funny. I guess I see past the skin color and look at what type of person they are. I know someone that gets discriminated against all the time. The person was raised in America. The mother is white and raised them as a single parent. Their dad is from Sadia Arabia. The person said you should've seen the looks they were getting when they went to the Airport. They have only met their dad a couple of times. IDK, it's not about what nationality they come from it's the person you have become. Just wanted to add something I learned about in Sunday school. You shouldn't follow anyone but Jesus. Everyone else will always let you down. They are only human. Only God will never let you down. There is not one person that does not sin. They will always fail you. No one is perfect. / There's a song I would Like for you to listen to. It's called "Where's the Love" by Black Eye Pee. It has a little beat to it. They Made a remix for those of you who's scared of a little beat. / I would like to tell you about a movie I watched. I don't remember the name of it but it's about this "African American" preacher and he let his son take over the choir. Well, his son decided to reform one of the songs to rap. His dad was furious. He said he's not going to allow devil worship music in his church. In the end, he realized it's not the type of music it is, it's what the words say. My son Joshua just told me the name, "Let it shine".

Chapter 26: Songs

There are songs that make you love everyone and songs that make you hate everyone. You want to hear something funny. I forgot and left my walker. I walked around the house three times looking for my walker. Who needs that stupid walker anyways? /I really enjoy my Sunday School Class, The Harvester Class. Bro. Keith Gainnie is the teacher. He always knows just what to say. He makes up a wheel of fortune for every lesson. This is what he had for the wheel of fortune. Oh, I forgot, and I even asked him after church. It was something like it's foolish to make Sunday your funday. It's kind of hits close to home considering I have a temptation to go on the boat instead of going to church. That's why I need a boat of my own. Well, I can't help, they invite us out on a Sunday. I also can't help that going out on the boat is more fun than church. I love that song that goes "money can't buy you happiness, but it can buy me a boat". It's Buy Me A Boat by Chris Johnson. If we don't remember anything else, we remember the wheel of fortune. We had a substitute teacher for Sunday school class. Bro. Lee Baker said the oddest thing, he said God remodeled him. Funny I feel the same way God remodeled me. / When I come home from the hospital, I did home therapy. I had all sorts of people coming in and out of my house. Chuck ended up putting up video cameras. / I remember my home occupational therapist said I could hit people and it can be therapeutic. That was awesome! My left arm has stroke symptoms. It was very weak; you could hardly even feel it. My mom stayed with me Monday through Thursday. My mom has done so much for me. I am very blessed. My ex-sister-law Kim stayed with me for a while on Fridays. That was very helpful. Then I started going to Brooks where I started getting better. Only the therapy at first and then there was the day program. That was from 9 - 3 everyday Mon. through Thur. It was great! Not only did I have fun, I learned a lot too. I remember Beth Woolsey would come by the Therapy place and bring me lunch every now and then. That made all of the other students jealous. I know her from Mary Stringfellow. My mom and Beth worked for Mary when her mother needed help. She just kept in touch through the years. After I went to Brooks Rehab, I went to Brooks Clubhouse after I graduated from the day program. It was for people like me. I liked it. It was fun. I got to do all kinds of arts and crafts. I really liked Mona. But I quit going there when I started back at therapy. I was sad. I did therapy 3 days a week for a while. I started staying by myself after my therapy was up. I'm happy I could stay by myself! My mom stayed with me until my therapy stopped. She said

I fired her but really, I just didn't need her anymore. That's better than how she usually loses a job. She takes care of people until they die.

I just want to say individuals that work in children's hospitals are very special. I don't think I could work with children that are sick or dying. I just couldn't, it would be too heart breaking. I would like to say thank you, you are very special. I think I'm going to donate to St. Judes. The last thing parents need during a time like that is financial problems. Neumers is really good too. That's what we have in Jacksonville, Florida. We had a missionary at our church. Mr. & Mrs. Watkins. They are missionaries to Costa Rica. He was a major league baseball player. He didn't want to be a preacher. Well, he was called to be a preacher, she was called to be a missionary. Long story short, he didn't think he could get anymore happy. He was already living his dream. Well God gave him a warning. I believe in warnings, remember that story about Jonah and the whale. He (Mr. Watkins) went from being in the major leagues to living in his mother- in-law's basement with his family. He said one warning was enough. But the strangest thing, he said he is happier now than he has ever been in the past. He also said there are three types of Christians. A cold Christian. I used to be a cold Christian before my accident. I blended in with the non-Christian. If you saw me, you wouldn't know I was even a Christian. Then there is the warm Christian. They are the ones that cause a problem. There like me, now. They go to church but outside of church you can't tell the difference, or I believe in one thing because that is what the Bible says but I don't follow through with it or do it. I am a warm Christian. I cuss and do bad things like I lie. I am a warm Christian. Then there are hot Christians. That is what I would like to be. I guess what I am trying to say is your past is your past. You can't judge people on their past just on their present and future. Anyone can change. I want to be a hot Christian. I want people to look at me and think that's a good Christian. I want to do whatever God wants me to do. I want to be like Jesus. / I remember Lisa telling me if something looks unsafe then don't do it. It's sort of like my new motto, know your limitations. Words I live by now.

Jesus likes using sinful people. He cleans dirty people up and uses them. He used Paul and Paul was a murder. He used to have people stoned to death. He later became one of the most well-known preachers ever. / I wanted to say that cancer has affected a lot of people I know and care about. Some ending in tragedy. Some end in good terms. Thanks to technology. And my very favorite unexplainable healing. That is when You know Jesus is in control. I would like to donate to the cancer society. / I came across this on Facebook. "TBI -instead of (traumatic brain injury) its "to be inspired." I think it fits me to a T. I believe that deep down inside I am destined to do great things. Since my accident I think I can do anything.

That's not true. I was always somewhat like that but not as bad. I definitely wasn't into remodeling my house. I wasn't at home all day before so now I'm home during the day I can watch HGTV. I can't watch it when Chuck gets home. / I'm going to do my Journal now. Then you will truly see why I said my life is too boring to talk about. I hope to find the name of the doctor that told me to write a book, without him this book would not have happened. I would like to tell him thank you.

Chapter 27: Journal

Journal

4-27- 14 Today was a good day. I had my last PT apt. I did good then 2 see Dr. McCollic. I'm kind of upset I still need my walker. But it's all in the Lords own time.

- Pages ripped

5-8-14 Well today is Monday. Saturday was a great day. RayRay was here. Ashley, Red &

Aubreilla came over for Reds b-day dinner. So, did Miranda, Mike, Morgan & Bree and let's not forget Caleb. Chuck and Ashley did a great job on dinner. We even had a fire afterwards.

Bree name is actually Aubree

Sunday wasn't that great. I didn't go to church and I was so looking forward to it. I'll probably never get him to go to church either. I found out first thing I'm probably not going to the gym. I guess I am a SPIA (spolt pain in the A). I hate when I plan on something it doesn't work out. Well, I'm going to go for now. Bye. Oh, I just found out I get to go to the gym today. Yeah

I am not good at keep a journal. I am noticing I don't write in here a lot.

5-9-14 2day was a good day. I did all my exercises, but I didn't do my chores, but I'll do them 2morrow. We are watching Aubriella 2night. I love her so much, my grandchild. We rented Frozen 4 her. Ashley & Red took Joshua and Noah 2 see the movie Captain America. Chuck is fixing the golf cart. Hopefully we get it fixed tonight. Now we are going 4 a golf cart ride. Me, Chuck and Aubriella. She is going to spend the night too. We will have her until 2morrow night. Joshua is gonna be so happy the golf cart is fixed. Well, I wrote enough for 2night. Later

I had more written, but I couldn't read it.

5-12-14 2-day was a crappy day. I tried 2 do the balloon yarn ball craft project. It did not turn out well. I made a huge mess. I took a nap and got up 2 clean it up. I also tried 2 clean the floors but it was too hard. I couldn't do it. Having TBI sucks. Ashley's b-day is 2day and she didn't even come over.

5-13-14 I fixed supper with Joshua's help. Meatloaf is what's for dinner. Let's put it on Facebook. (JK). I dropped the meatloaf in the oven.

I did have more wrote but I couldn't read it.

5-20-14 Well it's been a few days. We had Joshua's b-day party Saturday at Rebounders. Then Ashley, Katie, and Aubriella came over. We grilled out. It was an awesome day. Then Mother's Day. It was awesome too. Then Monday, which is 2day, I went 2 the gym and then Ashley come over then we took mom to Red Lobster, Yummy, my favorite. Now we're chillaxin. Well, it's time 4 bed in a little bit. Night

5-31-14 2day is going 2 be a good day. Ashley is coming over with Aubriella and Katie. We are going swimming. Man, I got to buy a gift for Cory's graduation party tonight. I need more sleeping pills. I woke up at 3 AM. I took 3 different times 3 melatonin's. That's 9 in total. Still didn't go back 2 sleep. It's only 8:30 AM and I've already eaten breakfast and written in this journal on a Saturday. Valorie is supposed 2 come and visit for a week tomorrow. Well, I guess we are going swimming.

6-8-14 Well it's been 5 days since I was on here. It's a Saturday. Well let's see, Thursday I went 2 the gym. I got a good workout. Friday after my nap I went in the pool. 2day after my nap I yelled at Chuck. I shouldn't have yelled at him for wanting 2 go in the pool. So, he didn't have 2 put me on the treadmill. I am not going in the pool. As punishment 2 myself I'm going 2 walk an extra 15 minutes on my treadmill. I walked 1 ½ miles. Now I'm gonna have 2 do that every time. Before my nap Ashley took me to Party City 2 buy decorations 4 her baby shower. We also looked at decorations for Aubriella's birthday party. We had so much fun. Now I'm watching Fast and Furious 6. It was really good with the Rock and VanDisel. Next, we took Joshua for football tryouts. RayRay came over this weekend 2. I'd have to say it's been a pretty good weekend. Chuck is cooking hamburgers on the grill.

It's funny how some things in my journal I can remember like it was yesterday and some things no matter how hard I try I can't seem 2 remember.

6-11-14 Well yesterday I met Sue & Tonnie at the Women's Club. Wouldn't you know, no one was there. But even though we couldn't go inside we got a lot accomplished. 2day, I was supposed to go 2 the gym but mom chickened out. Well Mike moved in today. ttyl

6-21-14 Well today is a bad day. First, I spilt a cup tea all over the counter. Then Dana's being a slacker and were not having spin again (she said there's not enough people). I dropped the coffee creamer out of the fridge and on 2 the floor.

- Page ripped off

7-1-14 Well 2day is going a little better. I went 2 the gym. Well that's the first time I got stuck in my room, the wheel came off my walker and I didn't want 2 mess the floors up.

- Can't read.

7-14-14 Well I have no spinn again today. Dana's being a slacker for real. She has yet another excuse. Linda and Terry weren't there. Wait that's kind of the same excuse as last time, not enough people.

"can't read".

Trying to set up Destiny's b-day party around Ashley's baby shower. It's a big hassle. Then I took a nap, and walked on the treadmill. Don't tell Chuck. He'll get mad me walking on the treadmill without a harness. Miranda took me get outfits 4 the sign in picture photo. Now, Mike invited his family over, yeah. And the other Mike is coming over 2.

Chapter 28: The better me

After Journal:

I couldn't find the name of that doctor. I just wanted to say thank you to him anyway. I think it was Dr. McCollic. Without him this book wouldn't have happened. / I wanted to thank everyone for sticking with me through the boring part, the journal. I am thankful for Chuck losing my journals and the fact that I can't read my own handwriting, right now anyway. Also, some of the pages were ripped out. That made the journal portion shorter. It was really the boring part. I couldn't imagine how boring this book would be if I tried to put all of my journals in here. I have to be honest. I erased part of my journal. / I can't believe some of the things I talked about before my journal. I talked about wanting to keep my bust and lose weight, basically my stomach. I am embarrassed and ashamed. I could of easily have taken it out, but I wanted to show everyone how much I've changed during the process of this book.

 I also just got to say I am cool! I know I said a handicap isn't cool, but I was wrong. I'm the coolest handicap I know. A friend once told me it's all according to who is looking at you. One person's idea of cool might be different than another's. I am cool. I'm the 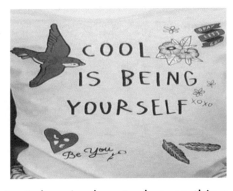 only person I know that can almost die in a car accident, was in hospice to learning how to do everything all over again to becoming an author of my very own book. Matter fact I am the only person I've heard of that was admitted to hospice and come out alive. I still have a walker. I need to figure out how to get rid of that. All in the Lord's own time. If I have to use the walker for the rest of my life, I'll be happy. Not satisfied but happy. I'll never quit trying but happy I'll be. / As shameful as it sounds, I'm not sure if I would have been friends with myself before the accident. I would like to think I'm not that shallow, but you never know how you're going to act in a situation until you are in it. / I also wouldn't beat up

Chuck if he cheated on me. See I have the "I don't hit girls" thing going for me. I would try (no promises) to buy him a condo and let karma handle it. I believe that karma is God. I also would of never have been able to be a testimony for God.

I decided that I don't want to go back to school to be a physical therapist. I'm old enough already after two-years of school, I'll be ready to retire. It's a woman's prerogative to change her mind. School was

hard enough before the accident and my TBI and I think it's time for me to relax and travel. With my Missionaries need nice houses too foundation I'll be traveling all around the world. I might just get two gym memberships, one for me and one for maybe Lisa at planet fitness or LA fitness, I have a LA fitness by my house. I've always wanted to try it out. I'd also maybe get one where I can bring

a friend. Bring, like Lisa. I'd also have her to teach me how to wake board. Maybe get Nikki to come to my house once a week to teach me how to walk with no walker. I'll still do the water aerobics and art day. I'd get top notch security. / I also am not mean. A guy that was drinking once told me that if he says it while he's drinking it doesn't count because he doesn't remember it. Well, if a drunk guy can use it, I should be able to, I do have a traumatic brain injury you know. If I don't remember it, it doesn't count. I don't remember much that just happened, so I am a nice person. Ha, I like that! / Also, I'm not untouchable. I think my head was way too big. God put me in this world, and he can take me out. I'm glad God has never given up on me, the lord knows the awful things I have done. Mold me into what you want me to be, Lord. I love that children's church song that goes something like this "He is the potter I am the clay". I'm not sure of what the name of it is.

I would have never thought Chuck would have stuck with me and done all he has before the accident. I found out first-hand he'll stay with me through anything. I can't get rid of him, JK, I wouldn't want too. He is a very particular man. I'm proud to say that I've been keeping up with my job while Chucks been away, as a housewife and a mother. That still cracks me up, my job. Weekly house cleaning would be great. Just saying. That would make me & Chuck happy. / Oh yeah, I want one of them iRobot Rumba vacuum. Where you can set it to go off twice a week at certain time and it will do the hard floors along with the carpets. It figures out a pattern and will go all around and go back on the charger when it's done. That would be so awesome. Now, I want a Ion Shark Robot. They have a mop like that too. I want one that mops too. I also really want one of them google home mini things that they just started to advertise on TV. They also have something like that, that's called an Echo. There really cool. Idk, I hope it can understand me, I got one of them remotes that you talk into. Half the time it understands me and half the time it doesn't. Maybe I can get Ceil, my main speech therapist, to give me some more speech lessons so the home mini thing and everyone else watching my blog can understand me. My house is going to be technical. There was a thing I think it was on Flip Flop. It was a computer-generated laser light thing, like a computer on your wall. I want one. Aubreilla would love that. My house in Lakeland will be technical too. I can't go from being overly technical in Jacksonville to not technical at all in Lakeland.

Chapter 29: My job

My mom always says, "Everything should have a place, and everything should go in its place". Our house and everyday life has to have order to function in harmony. Where order begins is in your heart. You get order when you put confusion and disaster at his feet and then he makes something beautiful out of your life. / Chuck still wants me to do my so-called job, that still cracks me up. He even wants the toilet paper on the holder a certain way. I know it goes over the top but sometimes you just don't think about it. Do you want me to fold it up in a triangle at the bottom too? Like a hotel. I do have to admit I'm not as anal with the house when Chucks gone. He's a little more anal than me. My mom too, she's been coming over a lot lately. My job is considered occupational therapy. My job is making me better. I get faster at it every time I do it. So once again, I just do it, like Nike says! / I'm kind of glad I got in a car accident. I would have never been an Author of my own book if I didn't. I would never have gotten right with the Lord. I have gotten to be a witness to the Lord. I am honored. I would never have gotten my remodel. Well, that hasn't happened yet. I don't get that until I finish writing my book and get it published. I seem to be more appreciative of what I do have. I feel very fortunate now. God has spoiled me. I have everything I want and need at my fingertips. I have a beautiful house even without what I claim to know. I wouldn't lose faith. Don't get me wrong God has blessed me with what I have.

I don't actually hear voices. Believe it or not, it helps. Whatever works. A little shot out but not crazy. No matter what Chuck says. Everyone thinks I'm crazy, with all the things I claim to know. With God all things are possible. In the eyes of the world all Christians are crazy. Another thing I hate not being able to do is sleep when I want to sleep. Insomnia is truly a terrible thing. I just lay there in the middle of the night and think. That's when I get the best ideas for my book or anything really. That's why I can't sleep. My mind is still running. I think too much. / I hate not being able to talk where people can understand me. People usually just don't act like they even hear me at all. It's so frustrating. Then I decide I need to say something, and I can't control my emotions, so everyone thinks I'm really mad. It's a mess. I did it again, now everybody is mad at me, great. I can't even express myself. It's a shame of the things I am used to. Like I am used to hitting my head when I bend down. That also might give me another TBI.

My doctor called my pharmacist and sent a letter home. "Take medication as prescribed. You don't get to pick and choose what to take". I went home and googled my medications. It said for Zoloft (my antidepressant) that if start and stop often it can lead to suicidal tendencies. Guess I don't know what I'm doing, But, for real, I've never had a suicidal thought in my life. I guess, I'm going to take anti-depressants again. I'm not a doctor. I shall do what the doctor orders. It's bad enough having to worry about the medication doing you harm now I have to worry about killing myself. / Before the accident I didn't like sweets. I love them now. I don't just love sweets; I love all food. Well, I shouldn't say I didn't like sweets. I liked them; I just didn't crave them like I do now. Now, what do I have all around my computer, junk food. You should see me. I've got Reese's, donuts, cheese it's, cinnamon toast crunch treats, rice crispy treats, banana bread muffins, nuts, fruit bites, yogurt fruit snacks. You name it I got it. I'm doing my editing and I keep all these sweets to snack on by my computer. I'll look at the food and it's like it's calling out to me "eat me". I need to stop buying them. / I am considering fasting. Jesus fasted in the Bible. It might help me get closer to him and they say it's good to start a diet after you fasted for three days. Cleans out your system. / I hate not being able to sleep. I take Temazepam at bedtime then I wake up to use the bathroom somewhere between 12 and 3. I'll go back to bed, and I'll just lay there with me, myself and I.

Let me tell you Miss Reilly loves her Nana. I'm like her favorite person. Well, when I'm around it's all about me. She even looks just like me. She has curly light brown hair and the prettiest blue eyes you ever did see. She'll get my glasses. And where it used to be sunglasses it's now reading glasses. She puts them on top of her head like me. That's why I go through so many. She even gives piggy kisses. She is like my mini me. She is tough like her Nana too. She was in her car seat and Jimmie wasn't. We were still parked in the driveway. But anyway, suddenly, I heard a big scream. She bit the tar out of him. He had a big bite mark on his arm. They fight all the time now. She doesn't always win but she gives him a run for his money. She'll say, "stop it". In that sweet voice of hers. Reilly and I play fight a lot. I'll lightly start poking her and she'll get so mad and say Meany. She actually says memy. She'll lightly start hitting me and I'll lightly start hitting her back. She gets so mad. She is older now and now she stills my walker and turn and look at me and go ah ha a ha ha. That cute little bugger. She is already walking. I'm jealous, or as my daughter would say I'm jelly. I thought we would be learning to walk together. Jimmie still stills my walker too. My new fancy walker has a seat on it. We will be outside and he'll still my walker and take it to the other side of the yard and put the seat down and sit and watch all the kids swing. Don't worry, they always make sure he gives it back. I feel bad for Ashley. She has to deal with all three of them. Well, the two girls don't fight that much but both of them fight with Jimmie. I used to hate Ray and Ashley fighting all the time, only my parents would keep them together.

What can I say about little Aubreilla? She's so pretty and smart. She's the head of her class at school. The teacher's pet. She's a little spoiled, but I don't think there's anything wrong with that. If she's appreciative then it's all good. I taught Jimmie and Reilly how to drink from a straw. Aubreilla already new how to drink from a straw. They all know that they can have some of nana's drink. Because Reilly went through this stage where she called everyone mommy, I taught her this song. "Nana nana booboo" I only said the last part one time, "stick your head in do do". Ashley said real stern "MOM". Needless to say, I didn't do that anymore. She's got that mom look. I guess I am like a kid. I don't mean to be, but I guess I am though. / Now I am saying 2018. I'm going to have the best body of my life. It is still 2017 but who am I kidding it's too late to have the best body of my life. I am going to start a weight loss program on my blog, if anyone wants to join me. I'll give a prize to whoever wins. I know this when I get finished writing my book I'm going to get in shape. I might even fast for three days. / I got to be realistic. Some people don't think I can be realistic about anything. I try to look at everything realistically. Like my house remodel. I know that everything I want to do can be done. Everyone is always going around trying to find something that isn't possible. / Jimmie is so cute. He loves hot dogs. I always keep hot dogs around. Anyway, Ashley asked him if he wanted a hot dog and held it out to him. He got this look on his face like love and admiration and he said beautiful. I tell you the look he gives sometimes is something else. BOL.

Chapter 30: Don't judge an establishment over one bad visit

Well Orange Park hospital redeemed themselves. I was in the laundry room and I fell. Well, the front fell off my washing machine. I cut my back falling on my washing machine. We had to call an ambulance. I would like a moment to brag about my son, Joshua. He stayed calm and held a rag over it until the ambulance got there. They took me to OrangePark Hospital. They were nice, quick and very efficient. I was very satisfied. That just goes to show you that you can't judge an establishment over one bad visit. IDK though, being sent to die at hospice is hard to get over. I hope you don't mind if I go to my own doctor to get the stitches out, Dr. Alvarez. I would like to tell that nurse I did go swimming. She was very stern with me about not going swimming. My man went out and bought me some waterproof Band-Aids. What can I say I am spoiled? My daughter came home and cut up a pool noodle and put it over the edges of the washing machine. I guess I need to buy a new washing machine. I have such a good daughter. All my grandchildren say please and thank you and no sir and yes mam. It's so cute when you hear a one-year-old tell you that. Sip please and thank you, they all know they can have some of Nana's drink. / Little Jimmie he's so cute and bossy. He'll tell me in as deepest voice a two-year-old can have. "No Nana". When I'm picking on Rylee, Bossy little fellow. Only I can mess with my sister. He's really a good boy. He does get into everything, but he isn't that mean. What boy doesn't fight with his sister. He's very caring.

Check out my blog is completely free. See never seen before footage of my cruise to the Caribbean's. You get to see me go on a zip line and lots of other offshore conversions. I have heard publishing a book is really hard. That is why I decided to do my own audio. You can hear my expression and you can hear how stupid I sound. I'm not supposed to say that but, oh well. I'm not that good at following orders. It's good speech therapy. I will put in definitions for the harder words I used, plus I'll have texting terms too. What I have in this book plus other ones. Who knows I might just learn something new, and the day won't be wasted? I'm going to put a playlist for all the songs I listed in my book plus other songs I like. My first subject on my blog will be whether I should get a tummy tuck. I have concluded that my stomach isn't going anywhere. I have done so many sit-ups, it's unreal. Unless I get my stomach sucked out like a vacuum it's never going to be flat. But I do have mixed feelings on the subject. First, I think you should be happy with what the good Lord gave you. Second, I think he gave doctors the ability to do awesome things, why not use it. I guess it would be different if it was affecting my health but it's not. I do have high cholesterol. Maybe I'm just using that as an excuse. IDK, we'll see. That's where the Air Fryer oven would come in very handy. It bakes, hydrates, and does rotisseries. I can even make kababs with it. I want one. The second is whether I should get any tattoos. I have always wanted one. My dad said it states in the Bible that you shouldn't get permanent markings on your body, but I can't find it. I think (not sure) he said it was in Leviticus. I can't find it. I personally don't like a whole bunch of them, and I am told they are addicting. So, I have come up with a strategy that will make me stop. My last one I would like to get it on top of my foot. I want one there and that's supposed to be pretty painful, I won't get anymore. Even if the Bible says you should not have them, you can still go to heaven. The Bible does say that everyone sins. You can still be the nicest person or the meanest and still go to heaven. I've noticed people are having a problem understanding me, so I will have a computer-generated voice do another audio that way you can choose, plus I will say a few words that way they will get the same effect. It will be high tech. I will have two audios and five different types of good music, definitions, plus texting terms. For those of you that can actually read the book will be there too.

My mom saw a printed piece of paper with notes I've made for my book. Anyway, I had on it how mom and dad aren't going to be happy with me and my book and how I was going to give a new meaning to the word independent Baptist. So, she asked me about it. I just thought that sounded good, IDK. I told her that the only thing I disagree with is the drinking. Didn't Jesus turn water into wine? Mom says Baptist people believe it wasn't fermented. The Bible does say something about you shouldn't stumble. That means it was fermented. It also says that one glass a day is good for you and it's a proven fact that one glass of red wine a day is considered good for you. I think the bible said something about not having a habit and being drunk in public. I don't know where in the Bible that is located. Someone very knowledgeable of the Bible told me that and someone I trust. I am not that knowledgeable of the Bible. In 1st Timothy 2:8 it says you should not give in to too much wine. Please don't start drinking because of me, I would feel terrible. I agree with one thing Pastor Addair said about it "Nothing good comes from drinking". Well, some people get more sociable but then you take a risk of becoming an alcoholic. So, it looks to me the bad outweighs the good. / I may be wrong about this, but I think addictions are a sickness. Again, this is not a proven fact. I do have a traumatic brain injury. What do I know? I saw something on Face Book it said `addiction starts with a choice. That is why it's not an addiction". What about alcoholism? That's not illegal, but yet it can be an addiction. Also, what about pain pills your doctor prescribes you. People need that to function.

Chapter 31: I'm pro Madd

I am pro MADD. I don't think you should drink a lot where you are falling down slurring your words and all, but I don't think one or two glasses is bad. Again, know your limitations. I personally say if it changes you or how you would normally act then don't drink. Or if you're an alcoholic then fix the problem. I personally had gone 3 months without drinking before my accident. I know one person it made mean. If it makes you mean, I think you should fix the problem. If it changes how, you will normally act, then don't drink. I haven't found anything else I disagree with. I don't condone any kind of sin, drinking or not. I have to admit I've been past my limit. Other than being promiscuous and a little sloppy I still had the same moral values. I really kind of feel bad putting this in I was taught my whole life that Jesus doesn't like for you to drink. I have thought a lot about this. I even dreamed about it. I'm not just saying it because I want it to be true. Now please don't go out and start drinking because of me. I would feel terrible. I do have to admit that it makes people do some pretty stupid stuff sometimes. It does everyone differently. I believe he wants us to be happy. Definitely not saying you need alcohol to be happy, but it makes me giggly. Just saying.

I don't actually hear voices. Believe it or not, it helps. Whatever works. A little shot out but not crazy. No matter what Chuck says. Everyone thinks I'm crazy, with all the things I claim to know. With God all things are possible. In the eyes of the world all Christians are crazy. Another thing I hate not being able to do is sleep when I want to sleep. Insomnia is truly a terrible thing. I just lay there in the middle of the night and think. That's when I get the best ideas for my book or anything really. That's why I can't sleep. My mind is still running. I think too much. / I hate not being able to talk where people can understand me. People usually just don't act like they even hear me at all. It's so frustrating. Then I decide I need to say something, and I can't control my emotions, so everyone thinks I'm really mad. It's a mess. I did it again, now everybody is mad at me, great. I can't even express myself. It's a shame of the things I am used to. Like I am used to hitting my head when I bend down. That also might give me another TBI.

I got to be realistic. Some people don't think I can be realistic about anything. I try to look at everything realistically. Like my house remodel. I know that everything I want to do can be done. Everyone is always going around trying to find something that isn't possible. / Jimmie is so cute. He loves hot dogs.

I always keep hot dogs around. Anyway, Ashley asked him if he wanted a hot dog and held it out to him. He got this look on his face like love and admiration and he said beautiful. I tell you the look he gives sometimes is something else. BOL. All my grandchildren say please and thank you and no sir and yes mam. It's so cute when you hear a one-year-old tell you that. Sip please and thank you, they all know they can have some of Nana's drink. / Little Jimmie he's so cute and bossy. He'll tell me in the deepest voice a two-year-old can have. "No Nana". When I'm picking on Rylee, Bossy little fellow. Only I can mess with my sister. He's really a good boy. He does get into everything, but he isn't that mean. What boy doesn't fight with his sister. He's very caring.

Chapter 32: Check out my blog

Check out my blog is completely free. See never seen before footage of my cruise to the Caribbean's. You get to see me go on a zip line and lots of other offshore conversions. I have heard publishing a book is really hard. That is why I decided to do my own audio. You can hear my expression and you can hear how stupid I sound. I'm not supposed to say that but, oh well. I'm not that good at following orders. It's good speech therapy. I will put in definitions for the harder words I used, plus I'll have texting terms too. What I have in this book plus other ones. Who knows I might just learn something new, and the day won't be wasted? I'm going to put a playlist for all the songs I listed in my book plus other songs I like. My first subject on my blog will be whether I should get a tummy tuck. I have concluded that my stomach isn't going anywhere. I have done so many sit-ups it's unreal. Unless I get my stomach sucked out like a vacuum it's never going to be flat. But I do have mixed feelings on the subject. First, I think you should be happy with what the good Lord gave you. Second, I think he gave doctors the ability to do awesome things, why not use it. I guess it would be different if it was affecting my health but it's not. I do have high cholesterol. Maybe I'm just using that as an excuse. IDK, we'll see. That's where the Chef Emeralds double door air fryer oven would come in very handy. It bakes, hydrates, and does rotisseries. I can even make kababs with it. I want one. The second is whether I should get any tattoos. I have always wanted one. My dad said it states in the Bible that you shouldn't get permanent markings on your body, but I can't find it. I think (not sure) he said it was in Leviticus. I can't find it. I personally don't like a whole bunch of them, and I am told they are addicting. So, I have come up with a strategy that will make me stop. My last one I would like to get it on top of my foot. I want one there and that's supposed to be pretty painful, I won't get anymore. Even if the Bible says you should not have them, you can still go to heaven. The Bible does say that everyone sins. You can still be the nicest person or the meanest and still go to heaven. I've noticed people are having a problem understanding me, so I will have a computer-generated voice do another audio that way you can choose, plus I will say a few words that way they will get the same effect. It will be high tech. I will have two audios and five different types of good music, definitions, plus texting terms. For those of you that can actually read the book will be there too.

I've been coughing, almost choking a lot lately. More than normal. Yes, sometimes it's when I eat or drink. I don't tuck my chin when I swallow. But sometimes I'm not doing anything. There's no reason for me to have one of my coughing fits. Along with my coughing fit comes another one of my problems. God gave doctor's the abilities to do wonderful things, why not use it. That just reminds me of a blog question I'm going to do. I think I might have come up with the answer even before my book gets published. But no matter how hard life might get I am happy. I might get frustrated with my life and all my disabilities, but I can honestly say I am happy. Chuck says I can't be happy. He sees how hard my life is. How everything is a challenge? He just doesn't understand God = Happiness. Maybe if he was living for the Lord, he would be happy. I don't get why I'm so happy. I'm happier now then I was before my accident and I'm a handicap. I have such a hard time doing everything. It's really hard to believe that I am happier now than I've ever been. I just don't get it. The Bible says don't sin. But what is sin? My pastor says if you have to ask it's probably sin. Love is more powerful than sin. God gave his only son to die on the cross for me and you. Now that's love. God needs us to love him. I personally don't focus on sin too much. God is about love. It doesn't matter what you have or have not done. God is about forgiveness.

Chapter 33: I try to be like Jesus

I just try to be like Jesus. Even though I'm not anything like Jesus. I try not to sin, but I do. I am only human. I believe we need spiritual discipline. The blood of Jesus cleanses you from all your wrongdoing. When you get saved, you feel giddy inside, because you are clean. But I don't always feel like a child of God. I know I am, but I don't always feel like I'm good enough. I just don't feel worthy. I believe we should strive to have a closer walk with the Lord. I personally go by the 10 commandments and whatever is in the Bible.

- Ten Commandments;
- 1. You shall have no other gods before me.
- 2. You shall make no idols.
- 3. You shall not take the name of the Lord your God in vain.
- 4. Keep the Sabbath day holy.
- 5. Honor your father and your mother.
- 6. You shall not commit adultery.
- 7. You should not murder
- 8. You shall not steal.
- 9. You shall not bear false witness against your neighbor.
- 10. You shall not covet.

It's located in Exodus 20: 1-17 and Deuteronomy 5.

I also just want to say I cuss. I think it is all about respect. Mom, I am sorry I know you didn't like the word suck and I used it anyway. There's nothing in the Bible about cussing and there is no law about it. Who says what a cuss word is anyway? No one likes to be cussed out. Well, I have to admit. There is one cuss word I like my girlfriends to call me. It rhymes with witch and it starts with a B. They tell me that when there jealous. I have to admit I like making them jealous. If I had my way all of them would be calling me that at some time. I would like all of them to call me when they see my house remodel. I cuss at Chuck a lot. It puts a little spice in our marriage and there's nothing wrong with putting spice in your marriage. I cuss with Red too. It always leaves a smile on his face. If it makes him happy then it can't be all that bad. You know me and happiness. I don't like to hear children cuss. IDK why it just seems to be disrespectful. Well, not school age kids. IDK, it's kind of cute hearing a toddler repeats what their parents say. Well, they are too little to know what it even means. It's cute when Jimmie calls his daddy a A-hole after getting a spanking. Well maybe not to the parent getting called that. I guess you need to let them know it's bad. I suppose you need to watch what you say around toddlers.

I believe in spare the rod spoil the child. That's what's wrong with most of the kids today. There's no respect. God says to spank your kids. In the world today, it's not politically correct to spank your kids. There's a difference between spanking and abusing them. I believe you should try to be like Jesus. I still sin but I can try. I don't think anyone looks good when every other word that comes out of their mouth is a cuss word. I really think you should act like Jesus. WWJD? What would Jesus Do? Whoever coined or patented that phrase is a very smart person? If everybody tried to live by that, the world would be a much better place. / I believe you can be a crackhead and turn to God and you can become clean, reformed. The second you look away you will become a crackhead again. Jesus is that powerful. Anyone can change. / I would like to talk about Sunday's best. I like getting all dressed up in dresses and stuff. I want to wear something that makes me look pretty. So, going to church just gives me an excuse. I know a lot of people who don't like wearing suits or dresses. Like Chuck for instance, he likes to wear jeans and shorts. I don't think you should wear jeans that are all worn out but really, wear what you feel comfortable wearing. Don't not go to church because you don't want to dress up.

I really love the movie "God is not dead II". I also love their theme song. I'm not sure what the name of it is but it goes God is not dead he's surely alive. My son Joshua just informed me that is the name. That movie says our God is the only God in our history books. Even the dates state that God is real, BC – before Christ and AC – after Christ. Jesus Christ is the most influential person there is. There is proof of his existence, proof of his crucifixion, and many people saw him after his crucifixion. The crucifixion is indisputable. There is a multitude of people that have seen him after his crucifixion. That means he was indeed resurrected. Our nation was founded under God. Our money has "In God we trust" printed on it. Even our pledge of allegiance has "One nation under God" in it. Try and tell me there isn't a God. Prayer seems to be the last thing people turn to when it should be the first. I don't think I would have made it if I hadn't had people from all over the world praying for me. Missionary's and all. Just so I don't get in trouble for plagiarism I got a lot of what I just said straight from the movie. The movie is about how a schoolteacher is trying to prove to the court that God is real and alive.

Now I'm doing the editing. I have a desk at the double windows in the lower part in my bedroom where the double doors are going to be. I stare out the window and daydream of what my backyard is going to look like when it's all said and done. I liked writing a book. I get to tell the whole world all about me. I hate, hate editing. I know hate is a strong word, but I really do hate it. I despise it. / One of my plans is working. I had so many plans it's not funny. There are not SMART plans though, not dependable. Chuck took out a home equity loan to do the outside area. He's put hardy board siding up, painted it and he put double doors in my bedroom. I even got to pick out the paint color. You go boy! *Do all the work you want. I'll* do my design around what he does. That will be less for me to do. Very good. He also wants bench-like storage for the rafts and stuff. / I hate that everyone treats me like a child. My son Joshua insists on riding my motorized cart out of the house. Like I can't do it or something. / Chuck still wants me to do my so called "job" but if he saw me doing my so called "job" he'd tell me to sit-down. I do my job when Chuck is at work. Why do you think he bought me that bell? So, he doesn't have to watch me do anything. I truly scare everyone when I try to do anything. But I know it's occupational therapy and the more I do it the better and faster I get at it. So once again I just do it like Nike says.

I guess I have to put this in. The Lords been working on my heart about something. Trust me, the Lord doesn't like you to ignore him. This is a touchy subject for me. Someone once told me the Bible says a man should not sleep with a man and a woman should not sleep with a woman. I have no idea where in the Bible it's located. If you know you can go on my blog and write the scripture down. I know a lot of people that have had at least one bisexual act. I previously heard that if your bisexual than it shows in your DNA. Well, if the Bible does say that then I can't go against it. I do know if you have or do you can still go to heaven. Everyone sins. No one is perfect, like Jesus. I have no idea where in the Bible it's located. If you know you can go on my blog and write the scripture down. My blog is I'MALIVEWITHTBI, WENDY My blog is supposed to be as non-religious as possible so try to keep it discrete Although, I have to say that I really do love me some hamburger Mary's. That place is so fun and has great food. I think everybody should be treated with respect.

Chapter 34: My God died for us

I have something else to say about these people who sacrifice their self to kill everyone else, for their so-called God, My God died for us. He sent his only son to die on the cross for our sins. God loves us that much. Jesus come as an infant that was born in someone else's barn and had nothing but a manger for a bed. He was a carpenter. He didn't live like the king he is. He is God the father, Jesus the son, and the Holy Spirit. He is the big three in one. He wants us all to have peace with each other and not fight and go to war with each other. God is love. Real love doesn't keep record of the wrong done to them. I have something to say about commandment #3. I don't say GD but what about good Lord and Lord have mercy. I've heard people say Jesus and all kinds of other things that could be taking the Lord's name in vain. I say Lordy a lot. Is that taking the Lord's name in vain? / I know my gift. Someone told me everyone has a gift. When I heard that, I thought and thought. I couldn't find it. Some people are given the power of song. Some people have beautiful voices, and they can sing. I used to love to sing. I never thought I could have a career at it. Good thing, I've been told by more than one person that I wasn't that good of a singer. I know a couple of people said how good it was to hear me sing again. Some people can cook really good. A master chef in a restaurant. I enjoy cooking but I'm not good enough to be a chef. I have the power of words. Most people can't understand me. Half the time you can't read my handwriting. But if I can text or type it, I have the power of words. I can make Chuck or Ashley mad at me and I'll text them something sappy and it will be all good. Well, anybody really. If I can text it or type it, I have the power of words. Words are important, and they hurt, I have learned that during the process of this book. / I also wanted to say something about naming your child Jesus or anything else that means Jesus, Lord or God. Everybody thinks their kid is perfect when they come out with five fingers and toes but for real, they're not. What a powerful name Jesus is. It's the name above all names. I just don't think you should name your child such a powerful and glorious name.

Just wanted to say I'm proud as punch that God is using me this way. I stole that from pastor Adear. He says that or happy but I'm saying proud because that's what I am, proud. I am happy that I am living for the Lord. I never thought I could be happy going to church before when I was backslidden but I am. Oh yeah, pastor Adear says happy as pie and proud as punch. Well, now I'm going to steal both of them. I'm proud as punch and happy as pie. I am also honored that I am being used as a testimony.

Jesus gives you excitement and joy. He has made me glad. / Someone that is very religious said if Jesus turns out to be not true, I will be the biggest fool of all time. It's all according to your perspective. You can look at almost anything differently. I think that there is no downfall from being a Christian. If you don't believe you will be scared of dying. A Christian looks forward to death. They may be afraid of how they're going to die but not afraid of death. I have personally lived through unexplainable things that has to be God. I don't know of anything else that believes in life after death so there would be just nothingness. We wouldn't feel like a fool because we wouldn't feel anything. It's all about what perspective you have and how you look at it. I think I have heard of people being reincarnated as an animal. That would be disappointing. Thinking you were going to heaven, and you woke up a dog or something. I guess it is all about perspective. I never thought of it like that.

There is something else that's been bothering me. The most evil man that I have ever met said to me that he is going to wait till his deathbed then get saved. Well, I believe that a murderer can get saved and I believe you can get saved on your death bed, but it really disturbs me to think that this evil man will be in heaven with me. He only wanted to wait so he could be evil until he dies. You can go on my blog and tell me what you think. Well, my blog is supposed to be as non-religious as possible so try to keep it discrete. / You know when I said the Lord is working on my heart about something else too. Well, I didn't listen. One thing for sure it's no one's fault but my own. I know no one thinks I'm going to finish my book now. That's okay too, I get to prove them all wrong. You want to know something weird. God help me when I was in trouble. There is no doubt. I was wrong, and God helped me. That reminds me of a wheel of fortune- Jesus doesn't send us away when we are good but draws us into his arms when we are not. I know other good fathers like that. God's grace and Mercy forgives all are bad behavior. I'm pretty sure the devil had a hand at this too. The devil is also working overtime on me and getting this book done. He doesn't want me to finish that's pretty apparent. I am a sinner that he is using for a testimony. That reminds me of a children's church song I use to sing "He's still working on me, to make me what I want to be". / I just realized something; I am a hypocrite. I thought a hypocrite was them holier than though people at church going around judging people. Which don't get me wrong, I've been known to judge people too. But I googled it, and I am indeed a hypocrite. I believe in the Bible, but I did just what the Bible tells me not to do. / I would like to say something about judging people. I see very Christian people judging people. Doesn't the bible tell you not to judge. In my notion that's more sinful than whatever they did especially if it's not in the Bible. / It's nice writing this book. I get to whine to the world about my problems and shout it from the mountain tops when I have good news.

It's like I'm talking to a friend. It's really unbelievable that I am so happy. Lord, please, please grant me patience. Good grief this process is taking me a lifetime. / It is what it is, is my new saying and I got this TBI thing. I say both of them phrases a lot. I also say very good a lot. IDK why, I just do.

Chapter 35: God = Happiness

You want to know what I learned while I was writing this book. Well, a whole lot, you wouldn't believe all I learned. I couldn't even believe it. If someone told me this, I would think there crazy and I believe with God all things are possible. I need to remember that when somebody else doesn't believe me. Trust me, it's just not time to tell you yet. I'll only tell you this, he wants you to be happy. God = happiness. I never thought I could be so happy being religious begore when I was back slidden, but I am. God has provided me with Red, that tattooed up boy with the name Jesus tattooed on his sleeve. Thank you Red, you are appreciated. He went to college for computers. Plus, they stay with me when Chuck is working out of town. He has to listen to me complaining or as he calls it squawking. I found out my daughter is very good with computer stuff also. God has provided me with everything I need.

I just want to say how much I love the Geek Squad at Best Buy, if it wasn't for them, I don't know if I could have finished this book. Red has to work all these long hours. He just doesn't have the time to fool with me all the time. Red was saying he didn't think people who wrote auto biographies did a part II. I told him I'm interesting enough that I can. He then said I thought that's what your blog is for. Well, he does have a valid point. That's something I'm going to have to think long and hard about. / I have decided to go to Nevada for the summer with Chuck. He has a job opportunity there. It's on the west border so right next to California. I can visit Las Vegas. I'm looking at it as a long vacation. The Lord only knows how bad I need one of those. I'm thinking it's a way of the Lord granting me patience. The Lord also did it again. Red is super busy with working all these overtime hours at work and his family (life basically). I felt bad asking him to do more for me, so he sent me this long-haired young man from church, D.J. McKendree. He is really smart and knows a lot about computers. Once again, the lord is good, he used a movie (The Shack) to help me. He also used another movie to help me. I don't remember the name of it but it's about this high school football coach. They were on a losing streak and then they turned to Jesus. They started winning every game until they won the state championship. His wife was also trying to get pregnant and couldn't. Well, finally she told Jesus that it's okay. I love you anyway and she ended up being pregnant. This hit close to home because I told Chuck that if what I so-called know about doesn't come true I would lose faith. It's weird how he uses a movie to help you. I just thought about something, I can sell merchandise on my blog for the "Missionaries need nice houses too" foundation.

I know I can get people from my church to volunteer to sing and I can sell CDs or whatever on my blog. That's a great idea. I can ask my pastor if I can set the church up for a home base. If you want to help out the "Missionary's Need Nice Houses Too" foundation you can send us some home-made items to sell on my blog. We need all the help we can get, this foundation isn't cheap, so if you can crochet, make jewelry or anything really, we can sell it on my blog. All proceeds will go to the foundation.

Chapter 36: I'm in Nevada

I am in Nevada, and I have been thinking, I just want to say I love it here. My pastor was saying that moving can cause depression. I am not depressed at all; this is truly God's country. It is beautiful here. There are mountains in every direction. We are in the valley. I even stopped taking my antidepressant (Zoloft), since I did that bad thing and Jesus helped me. When I said Jesus is working on my heart and I didn't listen. The best part about it is Chuck works five minutes from where we live. He comes home for lunch on most days. Even Joshua is doing much better. I fasted the first 3 days I was here. I wasn't any closer with Jesus and I didn't lose any weight. Matter fact I was so hungry; I ate everything I saw afterwards. I went on a see food diet. I have not made it to Las Vegas yet. Although I am looking forward to going to visit. I was always taught you shouldn't surround yourself with sinful things. I don't think you should not go somewhere because there is sin there. I think if God is in your thoughts, then the devil will get behind you and flee. Well, that's my opinion, what do I know I have a traumatic brain injury. My initial plan is to be with Chuck. To be by my husband's side, right where I belong. I would live here permanently but your family is what makes you happy. And I miss my kids and grandkids. Well, all my family actually. I wish I could have the best of both worlds. / I was at this celebration and this lady was talking to me and invited us to go to her church. If this woman wouldn't have invited me to go to her church, I would still be looking for a church to go to. It's a nondenominational church but they use the King James Version of the Bible. I just want to tell her thank you. You were being used by God. I just want to say how important it is to witness to people. But I was always turned off by Bible thumpers. That's what I thought a hypocrite was. They go around judging everything you do, preaching at you. I would always try to avoid people that made me feel bad for not living for the Lord. I don't want to make it where people don't want to be around me. I want people to look at me and just see the goodness. Sort of like what that guy at the Verizon store seen in me. The two churches are very different.

Not what they teach, it's the same. So far, at least. This church is little, my other one is big. This one has a big window behind the pulpit. It's great. I love it. You get to see God's beauty as they preach. There is a big mountain in the background. Last week I saw an eagle flying around. It was beautiful. I like it being small. You get to know everyone faster. I had my whole life to get to know everyone from my other church. As long as they believe in the same thing. I'm good.

The people in this church are not afraid to show their love for the Lord. They are excited to be a Christian and you can tell it too. I have a change of heart about a few things. The first thing I have a change of heart about is going to a Baptist Church. I believe as long as the church believes in God and the way you get to heaven is the same. Which is publicly believing in him and confess your sins and believe he has forgiven you of your sins and don't deny him. And get baptized, even though baptism doesn't get you to heaven. You are supposed to get baptized as a profession of your faith. The lord commands you to get Baptized. It's a symbol of you publicly pronouncing you are saved and God washing away your sins. If you're saved, you'll know, and no one will be able to tell you any difference. You might not feel like you are saved all the time, but you'll know in your heart you are. You will feel the power of his presence. I feel there are 3 keys to heaven; 1) THE BIBLE – do what the bible says 2) faith 3) prayer. Also, you have to pronounce publicly that you believe in him. The second thing is the King James version of the Bible. Don't get me wrong, I know that is accurate. They copied it straight from the concrete tablets that the men of the Bible wrote it on. But it's kind of hard to understand. I don't see anything wrong with someone else interpreting it for you. I've read the Bible when I was in my teens once and I didn't quite understand it. I've read it way more than once but not from front to back. Chuck says he has a hard time understanding it and he's the smartest person I know. As long as there just interpreting it and not changing the context I think it'll be okay, that's what I've been doing all my life. Idk, just maybe we don't need to dumb down the King James version we need to educate ourselves to understand it. For centuries there has been controversy over the translation of the King James version of the Bible. The majority of religions, which is about 90%, go off the King James version of the Bible. The minority, which is 10%, doesn't. Our nation was founded under the King James Bible. It is undisputable. If you want to learn more about the King James version of the Bible read Sam Gipp. The Bible is my textbook for life.

Chapter 37: control what you do with your mind

Your mind, you can control what you do with your mind, and you feed the winner. To be good and right, go by the bible. / I'm not that knowledgeable about religions. I don't really agree with Catholics. From what I know about it, they worship Mary. Not saying there is anything wrong with Mary. She is very special. But the way I look at it, is she is just a person God used to do a wonderful thing. I am being used by God to do a wonderful thing too and I definitely don't think people should worship me. I am not worthy. Which I do have to admit being a virgin and having baby Jesus is much better than writing a book. It's God that made it happen, if it wasn't for God, she would of never have gotten pregnant to begin with. I also don't believe you can get to heaven by good works. I think you should do good works it'll make the world a better place. But there are some religions that believe that's how you get to heaven. Well, I don't think that, for who so ever believeth in him shall not parish but have ever lasting life. That is what the Bible says people. Don't get me wrong I believe that there will be people of a whole bunch of different religions in heaven. Believe in me and thou shalt not parish but have ever lasting life.

Someone giving a testimony showed me how important it is to be patient. Stop and smell the roses. Here I am in this beautiful place, and I'm worried about finishing my book. I should be enjoying myself. Spending time with my family. / Also, I just want to say everyone has different views of the bible. Don't take my word for it. I'm a handicapped that has a traumatic brain injury. I'm not very knowledgeable of the Bible. Read it and make the interpretation for yourself. For example, some people disagree with me on the suicide thing. They said do not kill is in the commandments. So is though shall not take the lord's name in vain. Are you going to hell if you say GD. It's not your fault you are sick. God is Grace, mercy and peace. For mercy endures forever. Plus, John 3:16 again. Just because they kill their self doesn't mean they don't believe in him. Jesus died on the cross to forgive you of all your sins. It's all about perspective, the other thing is I'm not sure about this not doing anything on a Sunday because you should be at church. I believe church is important, but Chuck must work a lot on Sunday. I believe that God wants us to be happy and having family time makes you happy. Although his commandment does say "make the Sabbath day holy". It doesn't say you have to go to church. It just says make it holy some way. I may be wrong, but I think as long as you believe in him and have a good personal relationship with him, if you miss a Sunday, it shouldn't matter that much. Being a Deacon's daughter, we never missed church. If the doors were open, we were there. That was figurately speaking, of course. He didn't say you could not sin, or you had to go to church all the time. The most popular verse of all time John 3:16 For God so loved the world that he gave his only begotten son, that whosoever believeth in him should not perish but have everlasting life". Can't believe that someone with a traumatic brain injury can remember that. I also know all of Psalms 100. It's only five verses but still. I had to learn it in Sunday School, and I still remember it. Whosoever, what a glorious word. It means it doesn't matter what color your skin is, what nationality they come from. Whether you are rich or poor, it just doesn't matter. Anyone can go to heaven. All you have to do is believe and he makes it easy to believe. As far as I know Christianity is the only religion that has proof. It's kind of hard not to believe with all the concrete evidence. The Bible is a proven fact. They found the stone tablets of the historically proven fact. Jesus is a historical proven character and the evidence, real history. /There is one more thing I would like to bring up. I'm confused about one thing. There are some people that believe you don't have to go by the Old Testament, that with the new times the Old Testament doesn't apply. Idk I think there's a lot to learn from all the stories. IDK, I don't know that much about the bible. I don't want to be someone who doesn't want to believe even with undisputable evidence, but I don't believe that. But what do I know, I have a traumatic brain injury? Like I said before, everyone has different opinions and views of the Bible. /Oh, I love it, my new church is sending someone to get me every Sunday and Wednesday. I would just like to take a moment to thank the lady coming to get me. You are truly a blessing. I knew as soon as I walked through the door, that was the church I wanted to attend while I was here. I personally love going to church now. God does say surround yourself with Godly people. I believe that if you are a faithful and hot or even warm Christian you should want to go to church. I sin all the time and I know beyond a shadow of a doubt that I am saved. I try to be like Jesus but I'm not. Don't get me wrong, church is very important, but family time is important too. I used to not like going to church when I was backslidden. I would have never of thought I would be so happy going to church and being a good Christian. I used to think Christian music was torture. Now I love it. I think it's cool. I have had a life changing experience with God. No one can tell me there is not a God. When I was in my car accident, I could feel the power of the holy spirits presence. Like his arms around me keeping me safe. I don't get atheism. Atheism doesn't take away the pain, it just takes away the hope. If we evolved from monkeys, why are there still monkeys? Atheists believe in the big bang theory, well what did the big bang come from. Well, I believe everything comes from something. They also say the timing doesn't add up. Well, I don't think that's a good thing to go by. One day of the Lord's time can be a thousand years in our time.

Chapter 38: The Devil doesn't want me to finish

Now I have formatting problems with my word program. It's only one or two words per line. I'll copy and paste it and it will go back to the two words per line. Right in front of my eyes. I don't even have to touch anything. What's next? I tell you the devil doesn't want me to finish my book. I'm not saying everything is right but still. He doesn't want me to finish. It has been one thing after the next. / Christine also cooks for us. She's an awesome cook. / Well, he did it again. He used a movie to speak to me. The movie is "Hacksaw Ridge". One more Lord give me the power to save one more life. That's my new goal. It's funny I watched this movie before and didn't get much out of it. For one I wasn't all that into war movies. For two since my accident, I have to watch a movie over and over again before I can follow it all the way through. Sort of like reading the Bible, you get something new out of it every time you read it. I think when I get done with my book, I'm going to try to read it from front to back. Also, I just thought about something I am going to promote "He's alive". I know this guy from my other church that sings this song "He's alive" and he's a really good singer, Steve Doshier.

I found out that I am a vein person. I always thought that was a bad thing. I know that it's all from God. As long as you know who it comes from. I just think you should look your best. I know one time being vain actually help me make a good decision. I don't think I look all that good, especially since the accident. I also found out I am very humble. God gives grace to the humble. / Halloween has rolled around again. In honor of the new movie wonder woman. I am going to be wonder woman for Halloween. The glory giver wonderful Wendy wonder woman. There I go, being a big geek again. Since my accident I've always gone as super girl. Because that is how I felt, super but now I will be wonder woman. / I'm having one of them "feel like I am on top of the world" moments. / I just have to put in something else. My pastor now of my non-denominational church is showing me in the King James version of the Bible how healing is real. Now they don't knock people down hitting them on the forehead. They put oil on their heads like in the Bible, but they produce a scripture to back it up. Not sure where it is located but I think somewhere in 1st Timothy something. My other church doesn't believe in healing. I think it's all up to God. I don't think that you can heal

everyone, or no one would die of old age or cancer. It's all according to Gods will. I do think it's possible. Anything is possible through God. Can you imagine how populated the world would be if no one ever died? I believe that God is doing all the healing, but sometimes he uses someone else to do the work. I had a few different people try to heal me. It didn't work. Maybe someone special needs to do it, not saying them people aren't special. Also, they believe in talking in tongue. I agree with one thing they said about it. God knows what you're thinking. I just don't understand why you can't just think about it. Maybe I just don't understand or get the concept. They also have the same views as me on drinking. If you only have a little bit and don't go overboard. As long as you keep the same moral values and don't overdo it. It's all right. I have to wonder if I'm really a Baptist. I'm confused! I feel like a child that is lost. Well, there pretty much Baptist, they just go by what the Bible says not the Baptist counsel.

One of my caregivers moved away, she was a good caregiver too. She was very picky with the house. I would say anal, but I don't want to offend anyone. Now I get Christine 5 days a week. Plus, I did something bad. I am right next to all the shops and stores. I can ride my little scooter to the grocery store, well anywhere really. Even though it doesn't seem like it we are right next to main Street. I decided to take off by myself and I twisted my ankle, I had to go to get it checked out. It was all swollen and black and blue. Well anyway everything happens for a reason. Now Chuck thinks I need someone all the time. I get Christine 5 days a week now. That suits me just fine. Twisted ankle well worth it. / Summer is over, and Chuck will be here working on his job until next summer now. Joshua wants to stay so I will stay with my family. We went to the top of Lake Tahoe. Let me tell you that place is truly heavenly. I went ziplining again. They had a rope activity gym course there, now Joshua wants one. I told you he wants a lot. Even though we have a big yard, its only so big. So, I was thinking maybe the Ninja Warrior practice gym can have a rope section on it. I think I seen a rope section on the Ninja Warrior show. He also wants a half pike now he's into skate boarding. There's a skateboarding park right by our house in Nevada. So, Joshua has really gotten into it. / I think God uses old age, cancer and all these natural disasters and mass destructions to make the world less crowded. Can you imagine what the world would be like if no-one ever died? The world is getting terrible. Mass destruction is the new norm. It says in the Bible that in the end of times there would be lots of mass destructions.

Chapter 39: He has made me glad

I just wanted to add that I am truly happy. He has made me glad. God wants you to be happy. I was a brat and I really wanted a Go Pro video camera for my blog. I thought that if I pretended to be depressed, Chuck would go out and buy me one. I know, I'm so conniving. I couldn't even pretend to be depressed. But for some reason, I am happier than I've ever been in the past. I just can't figure it out. I have no reason to be happy. I had so many so-called friends I couldn't count. Every little thing I do is hard. I have so many reasons to be depressed and miserable. But I am truly happy. It's beyond me. I can't believe it, believing in him makes people happy. I used to be pretty and popular. Now, I struggle doing everything. My life is so hard. I have muscle deterioration in muscles that is just plain embarrassing. He gave doctors the ability to do awesome things, why not use it. That reminds me of a blog question I am going to do. I think I've come up with the answer before I even finished my book. I'm going to have to come up with new questions for my blog. You can still comment but I'm pretty sure I've made up my mind. On the tattoo thing I found in the Bible where it says that you shouldn't get any permanent markings. Google and that Bible study app is amazing. I think Instead I'm just going to get stickers to cover up the areas I want so it doesn't get spray tanned. I might get the same sticker in the opposite direction and some body paint. Back to my story, Wendy. Sorry I tend to get off track. Sometimes I just wish someone could go just one hour in my shoes. The only thing I can think of is it is God. I am happy now because he wants me to be.

I have a new caregiver again. I swear I change caregivers like I change clothes. That's figuratively speaking again, of course. This one is going to go to the gym with me and we're going to do water aerobics. I can finally get in shape now that I'm done with this book. I've been in Nevada for about 2 months, and I haven't exercised once. Trust me, I can tell. My balance isn't near as good. I wonder if I'm going to have to exercise all my life. It's been 5 years since my accident, and I get all wobbly every time I stop exercising. I guess I will be a fit old lady. She is also going to be my dieting partner. I have gained weight since I have been here. I'm not going to fast again that backfired but would like to diet. I used to think being religious was not cool. Now I look at things differently. I'm going to live in a mansion over a hilltop where the street is paved with gold. I'm going to be blinging. Just like the song. I will never grow old. There will be no pain or suffering. There will be no sickness or any financial problems.

No stress of any kind. It will be so cool. Sorry, but I look at things differently now. It's not cool to go to hell and be in fire and pain for eternity. I would imagine you would be all burnt up and gross looking. It is cool to go to heaven. Where you'll have everything, you want and need. The walls will be made up of precious gems. It's going to be beautiful. / I love, love the movie and the song I can only imagine. I can only imagine when I meet my savior face to face. It will be glorious. / People don't like Jesus and Christianity. It's not normal. They think we are crazy. / I have become like best friends with my new caregiver. We have a lot of fun together. I don't feel different with her either. I know she's my caregiver and I should feel different, but I don't. I know one time I forgot all about being handicapped. I probably would have hurt myself if one of my other friends hadn't been there. I don't have to even do my job here. My caregiver does most of the cleaning and cooking. Well, she admits she can't cook very good, but she takes good directions. I do what I do best and just supervise. But I am finding out the more I do the more time I get to do other stuff, like shopping, eating out, working out and site seeing. It's a beautiful place and there's a lot to see. I have it made here. Although I do miss my kids and grandkids. Well, all of my family really. I made a whole new set of friends. I am figuring out that friends can be sort of like your family. They can't replace your kids and grandkids, but they are sort of like your family. You tend to forgive your family faster. I know I am not being realistic, but I really want the best of both worlds. I have a new set of friends here and a great church. I know I'm not being realistic but that is what I want. I can't imagine my life without these people in it. I want the best in both worlds. I couldn't be happier.

Guess what, Gods done it again. There is this boy, Jessey Euller at my new church that is very smart. Anyway, he does all the sound and puts the words on the screen for the song and Bible verses. He is going to help me with all the technical stuff. Let me tell you God is good all the time and all the time God is good. He never lets you down. He's always got my back. You hear that Chuck; God has my back all the time. / Chuck said that we probably won't even go to Las Vegas. It's like a 10-hour drive. Instead, we'll probably go see the golden gate bridge. That will be cool too. / You all can say I'm crazy all you want, but I just got a high five from Chuck and I was bad. I guess I've been trying to be good and have been good for so long. They told Chuck that I would have a lot of outbursts. See saying stuff in your head actually works. Anyone can change. I did, and I have a medical condition that says I should have uncontrollable outbursts. Joshua wants to stay here for good or at least until he's out of school. There are too many bullies in Jacksonville. What are we going to do? I know Chuck wants to stay here too. I love it here. I've made a whole new life here. But I really miss my kids and grandkids. I know I can't have both. But my home is in Jacksonville where my house and family are. Oh, I have no idea what I'm going to do. I know I'm going to get my house remodeled. Now I'm sad. I' m going to miss everyone here in Nevada. What's going to happen, I really don't know. I know I get my house remodeled. Maybe I can have a bed and breakfast or a houseboat. I absolutely love that episode of fixer upper where they do the "Double Decker". I know we can have a houseboat on Lake Tahoe. I've always wanted a bed and breakfast in old St. Augustine anyway. Or maybe I'll give Chuck his condo. Now my imagination is going wild. But like I said before if you're going to dream, dream big. I guess I need to win the lottery. / We are going to have thanksgiving dinner with my new caregiver. It'll be great. She is sort of like my new family. Well, I have a change in plans for Thanksgiving. Instead, we decided to stay home, it'll be just us three and another young man who calls us his second mom and dad. See I can have a pretend family. I get to cook my famous stuffing and baked macaroni and cheese. My daughter and her family will be coming down for New Years. I get to see everyone.

Chapter 40: Opportunity makes a future

I did it again, I lost a pound, so I rewarded myself with a milkshake. I got to stop that. I'll never look the way I want to. / Opportunity makes a future. Look at me. If I wouldn't have got in a car accident, I wouldn't have been able to write this book. / In the Lords own time" means wait bitch. Sorry if I offended anyone. I thought it was funny. Oh, someone I trust just told me that the Bible says a cuss word is anytime you're not using the word in the right context (not to the right meaning). I guess I am not a female dog. I guess I did it again. Now I know why mom doesn't like the word suck. I just can't get it right. I told you; I am not a good example. Here I am telling the world with this book it is okay to cuss. I feel ashamed. I'm a good example to never look up to anyone but Jesus. I guess I'm going to have to get rid of the things I bought. I bought a cup and a little hand-held vacuum that are of a poop emoji and it says happens on it. Wait a minute I say that doesn't fly too well with me a lot. Is fly a cuss word. Now I'm confused again, great. All this Bible stuff is confusing. Maybe I'm just thinking too hard about it. I say a lot of words that have different meanings, and they are not considered to be cuss words. The poop does mean poop most of the time. And it's a cuss word either way. Well, I'm keeping the poop emoji things that has happened on it. That mini table vacuum comes in handy; I like it. Forgive me Lord for I have sinned once again. There I go, being a warm Christion again. I do know there is no sin too great for God to forgive. That's why I think it is very important to witness to people in prison. You can be a serial killer and still go to heaven. Your past is your past. You can't judge someone on their past, just on their present and future. I will change, is what I'm telling myself over and over in my head now. I believe that God doesn't focus on sin too much. He needs you to love him. God is about love and happiness. I believe if you're a hot Christian, you will want to be more like him, but God doesn't focus on that, WWJD again.

I still can't believe I'm so happy. My life is so hard, emotionally too not to mention the physical aspect. Emotionally this is the hardest thing I've ever had to go through. / I feel very fortunate and blessed. I see people every day that has disabilities and so much pain it's unreal. God has made it to where I don't have any pain. The only medication I am on is a Mobic for my arthritis and I take over the counter sleeping pills, I can usually go back to sleep if I wake up to use the bathroom. I'm always awake by 7 o'clock, usually earlier. If I am tired, I'll sleep! /"Never give up on a dream because of the time it will take to accomplish it. The time will pass anyway." That's one of Facebook sayings that I thought was relevant considering it's taking me such a long time writing this book. It's taking me longer to edit this book as it did to write it. Joshua is fifteen. He was 11 when I started this book in and the Patch the Pirates Club. Now they have the Awana Club. He's in the Youth Group now. He has already changed how he wants his room decorated. He wants it in black and red. Since I can't very well paint his room in black or red, I was thinking paint it in white and have black and red calligraphy on his walls, it would sort of be like graffiti on his walls. He's so good with the grandkids too. My grandkids are getting so big. Aubreilla is six fixing to be seven now and let me tell you she is getting so big and more beautiful every day. Jimmie is three fixing to be four and he was very little when I started this book. I was doing my journal when she had him. Rylee is two. Fixing to be three next week, she'll be three before I finish. Ashley had her while I was writing this book. She is like my mini me. I love her so much. Well, I love all my grandkids the same, but I think I'm closest to her. Well, she's closest to me, most definitely. Dana was pregnant when I started this book. Her little boy is the same age as Jimmie. Cliff and Michelle already had a baby girl since then they had another. I've been so wrapped up in this book, it's almost like I actually did die in that car accident. / I may be wrong, but I don't think you have to go to church to be a Christian. I believe if you are a hot or even a warm Christian you should want to go to Church. But some people aren't as fortunate as me to find a Church their comfortable in. I believe if you worship him in some way then it'll be okay. But never deny him.

There are new shows that have come on my HDTV station. Now my new favorite shows are, "Flip Flop, Fort Worth and Hometown. Let's not forget Desert Flip Flop with Linsey and Erik Bennet from Palm Springs. Who am I kidding, I like them all? And oh yeah, I can't forget" First Time Flippers" with Egypt Shirod. I'm not sure if you spell her last name like that but it sounds like that anyway. I really need to meet her. My vision is good, but I have no idea how to accomplish it. Let's face it, I know nothing about flipping a house. I don't even know the different styles of houses there are. I have a lot of learning to do. I know I can take designing courses for my Alzheimer's disease experiment. If I think for a second, I can come in this business and not know anything than I really am crazy. I figured out that the reason why I watch HDTV all the time is because I don't have to follow a story. I can look up and I know exactly what's going on. Plus, I'm really into it. / Sorry, it's taking what seems to be a lifetime to complete this book. I do have a traumatic Brain Injury you know. / Well, it is 2018 now, so now I guess I'm going to be saying 2019 I'm going to have the best body of my life. It's already May so I don't think I'm going to have the best body of my life. I can't get my tummy tuck till I get money for this book. / Let me tell you he sure likes trying your faith. It's taken such a long time getting this book published I'm even beginning to wonder if this is really going to happen. I do have faith though. I may be in a hurry, but God isn't.

God is very patient. I need to learn to be more patient. I can't very well work so all I have is time to kill. I would like it to be published for Joshua's sake. He'll only be living at home for three years, I guess. A lot of my remodel is for Joshua. I would like for him to get to enjoy it for a little while at least. There also are other people that seem to be more impatient than I am. If you can believe that. Patience is one of the many things I have to relearn. / There's something I have to confess. It's been eating at me for a while, I not only lied to my mom and Joshua my son, but I lied to the whole world with this book. I have never read the Bible from front to back. Don't get me wrong, I read it all the time. Just not from front to back. I guess I thought everyone would expect it out of me, but I can't go on lying to everyone, it's just not right. I would like to read it from front to back with the family. Me, Chuck, and Joshua. Like a family thing. I shouldn't hold my breath on Chuck. But at least me and Joshua. / Someone else is calling me ungrateful. Could it be true? Well, I do just expect people to do things for me and I expect everything to be a certain way. I guess I need to learn to be more grateful.

Chapter 41: It's okay not to be happy if you're going through a bad situation.

I figured out its okay not to be happy if you're going through a bad situation. It doesn't mean you're depressed. You would be kind of weird if you laughed when something happened. Come to think of it you would kind of be like me when I smile when I really want to cry. / I've been thinking, I know that's dangerous. My Church in Nevada was saying the in the end of times there would be some great women preachers. Well, if this isn't the end of time, I don't know what is. I believe Joyce Myers is one of the great women preachers. She was Just saying that Jesus (I think) had something tattooed on the palm of his hand. Well, if she can show me where it is located, I will be her tattoo partner. I've always wanted a few. We can go together and get tattoos. That's also one of my blog questions. Ok, that debate is still open for discussion. Remember my blog is supposed to be as nonreligious as possible. So, try to keep it discrete. / I just want to say I love the bathing suits they have now. They are like t-shirts and shorts, but very fitting and in a bathing suit like material. I have learned during the publishing of this book that money is indeed the root of all evil. I understand now. / Sometimes it can be a curse knowing things. Not everything I know about is good.

I'm really glad I went to church this morning. I feel much better. The substitute preacher, Brother Holden told us all about how faithful Job was. He had everything taken away was tormented in pain and never lost faith. Here I am, a pitiful sinner, with faith as small as a grain of a mustard seed and here God is using me to bring testimony to him. I am truly honored and so undeserving. I can't grasp of why he chose me. I am getting mad at God. For what? Saving my life, making me free from pain! I am mad at him for hurting my loved ones. You can hurt me all you want but don't hurt the ones I love. But all of Job's kids were killed and Job never lost his faith. I went back Sunday night; the teenagers had the whole service. We had Junior Baker and another young man preach on Job and a whole bunch of talented singers. Let me tell you they had these two girls; they did a special and let me tell you they were a blessing. One played the piano beautifully. Come to find out that she found a keyboard in someone's trash and brought it home and taught herself. I couldn't believe it. I took piano lessons when I was little, and I was pathetic. God gave that girl a gift and she should use it more. God talks to you differently than a person talks to you. He talks to me all the time: through his word the Bible, preaching, teaching, movies and songs. He can even talk to you in your sleep. He even talked to me by making little voices in my head that nobody hears but me. Well, I don't really hear voices. That does make me sound crazy. It's all in my mind, more like thoughts. Maybe I can get Dr. Phil to evaluate me to see if I'm certifiably crazy. I definitely know how Noah felt when he was building an ark when there hasn't been any rain. Everyone was ridiculing him. / Now, it's this stupid house. First, there was a roof leak. Then a water leak, all the floors were flooded. I have wood floors like laminate, stick together wood. So now they are all buckled. We figured out it's the hall bathroom tub so we all have to take turns in the master bath. No big deal. Then the water heater catches fire. Dream home my butt, it's trying to kill me. / I wanted to tell everyone that I still, even after me trying to change, don't pray before meals like I should. I also have caught myself saying God out of context. I didn't think I did that. / Also, I just want to say I pray all the time by just thinking, But I believe it is good to pray out loud. There are less distractions. / I was down in the dumps and my momma and daddy came and spoiled me a little and that's all it took. I am a SPIA for a reason. But they spoil me with love not materialistic things. I also can't be any more honored than I am right now. I am convinced that God himself is telling me what to put in my book. When I wake up at we hours in the morning thinking about what to write. I've never even heard of a lot of it. So, I haven't put it in my book yet. Let's face it, I'm not that knowledgeable of the Bible. So, I wait until I get some kind of proof. I'm not going to write about it. It stays in my mind until I get proof. Remember, I have a traumatic brain injury. I don't remember much, but I remember this. I go to church, and they teach or preach about it, or both. To me that's got to be God.

Chapter 42: I am so unworthy

I am so unworthy. I put God on the shelf for more than 20 years. If you saw me, you wouldn't even know I was a Christion. I definitely wouldn't have met Chuck if I was living for the Lord. I know someone asked me why after the accident I started to go to church and became so religious. It's because when I was in my accident I felt him, like the holy spirit wrapped his arms around me keeping me safe. I know my book is a little unorthodox but I'm all about being different. Be sure to log onto my blog. Make sure you subscribe. It's free; Go to u-tube I'MALIVEWITHTBI, WENDY. See if everything I so called "know" about comes true. For me it's not if it comes true it's when. See my house remodel. I plan to go on another cruise too. With me, you will get to see a handicap in her everyday life. U will get to see how I cook. So, you will also get a cooking portion. Even before my accident, I'm what they call a lazy cook. I cook very good, but nothing is really fresh. Well, some things are but I use already prepared sauces and noodles and soups. Even before my accident, I never cooked from scratch. I've been watching different people's u-tube blogs trying to learn what different people do. One lady opens up mail orders. I can do that. Well for me I forgot what I ordered so we'll be getting a surprise in the mail. It would be great. Also, one lady did hers on fashion. I love fashion. I can do that. Also, I will do one day a week on helpful hints. I will be taking you everywhere I go. If I really do start a Missionaries need nice houses too foundation, which I will, I will be taking you along with me. If I go house flipping for a living you will see that, which I will. I love vacations and I plan on taking a lot of them. I'm still not sure about part II of my book. That I'm still thinking about. I've had such a tough time I don't think I'll want to write a part 2. Plus, it puts a strain on mine and Chuck's relationship. That is the main thing I was talking about when I said I have emotional problems and let me tell you that's more hurtful than a car accident. Remember when I was joking, and I said I can't get rid of him. Well, I am very shameful to say I think it's the other way around. It's very odd, I always said I would never be like that. But I love him so much. I don't think I'll ever love like this again. I know he's a BAH for sure, but he's my BAH. I also don't think my eyes can take writing another book. I'm about blind as it is, not really (JK) but can see far away but my reading glasses don't even work good anymore, and I am starting to see double and blurry sometimes again. I can't even read text messages without concentration, and I can't even zip my clothes up without a hassle. I don't know how I'm even writing a book. I think that bothers me more than anything else. I have gotten used to the way "the new me" sounds. I still think I sound stupid, but it's been years. I guess I just got used to it. But the seeing thing. I don't know if I'll ever get used to that. Seeing is important.

Chapter 43: My grandkids are growing up

  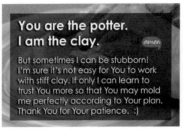 

My grandkids are growing up. It's taken such a long time: my brother Joel and his daughter Naomi drive a semi-truck now. I have my heart set on a metal roof and no one I know does metal roofs. David has passed me down to Jessi. Well, he's sort of like family. /Steve Harvey was at Disney World renewing these people's vowels. They gave them as a wedding present a trip to Hawaii to stay in the Disney resorts. That would be awesome. Matter fact when I get money for this book, I would like to get all the

kids and grandkids a trip on a Disney cruise. /Do you believe in miracles? I do, it's a miracle I was even able to write a book, with my dystonia and eye problems. Now they're saying CDs will be obsolete. Everything is through the cloud. I'm going to have to learn about that. The cloud thing is new to me. But I want what I want. Let me tell you God is good all the time, and all the time God is good. He is also very faithful. He's more faithful than anyone I know. Now I am getting a boy that I knew from before the accident, Raymond Seth III. I kept up with him through Face Book. He is a computer technician. I am going to get him to help me with the cloud stuff. They tell me the cloud is nothing but a really big computer in the sky. I'll have two audios', definitions, texting terms, and five different sections of diverse types of music. There is something else too I think you'll really enjoy. I am going to try to make it as simple as I can. Make sure you follow me on my blog, I'MALIVEWITHTBI. Find out whether I'm crazy or if God really did let me know what's going to happen. Go with me on all my vacations.

The guy that was supposed to be good with computers and the cloud isn't talking to me. Now it's time to let go and let Jesus take control. I love that song by Miranda Lambert "Jesus take the wheel". It's been a long time since I've written here. Well, I finished it and I tried to get it published but the money wasn't there. My dad went home to be with the Lord. It's okay. I get to spend eternity with him. The only thing he wanted for his funeral was Steve Dozier singing Bula land. And that's what he got. Joshua is 17 now. My grandkids are all in school. / I seem to watch way too many videos. See you get helpful hints when you watch videos. I get really high in the games because I have plenty of time to watch lots of videos. / I can brush my teeth without much problem, I can even open a can, but my life is very hard. I guess the New me does need a walker. Sorry Lisa. No-one minds if you say the black word now. Every time I eat, I start coughing, almost choking. Then I have yet another problem. I found over the counter products that pretty much help, but I will be thankful when I can get a medical procedure that will give me a permanent solution.

Right now, where in isolation from the Corona virus COVID -19. The world is coming to an end. It really freaks everyone out with me coughing all the time. It's the beginning of the end. He's coming back soon. So, if you're not ready, you better get ready before it's too late. This COVID-19 makes me sound like a liar. I've been trying not to lie. I'm not traveling anywhere anytime soon. I found out the longer you walk with Jesus and try to be like him the easier it is. I don't even think bad thoughts anymore. Well, I can't lie sometimes I do, I am definitely not perfect. Idk, if it wasn't for the second time God told me something, I would think I am crazy. But I can prove that it was true I just would like to keep the other party involved discreet. I haven't seen any of my friends in years. Either they all think I'm crazy or Chuck has done something to make them mad or maybe a little of both. / Pastor Adair son TR preached one day. What he said really made since. I believe happiness is a lot like joy. But happiness can be taken away from you in a bad situation. Bad things happen all the time that we cannot be happy about. But no one can take the joy of the lord from you. That's why I wasn't happy when my dad died or when I was going through a bad situation. Joy that's something nothing or no one can take away. Make sure you check out my blog. Remember don't text and drive and in the Lords own time means wait, wait, and wait longer. I hope the day wasn't wasted reading this book. Remember God & Jesus = love & Joy.

Printed in the United States
by Baker & Taylor Publisher Services